Fortress • 39

Russian Fortresses 1480–1682

Konstantin Nossov · Illustrated by Peter Dennis

Series Editors Marcus Cowper and Nikolai Bogdanovic

First published in 2006 by Osprey Publishing
Midland House, West Way, Botley, Oxford OX2 0PH, UK
443 Park Avenue South, New York, NY 10016, USA
E-mail: info@ospreypublishing.com

ISBN 1 84176 916 9

Cartography: Map Studio Ltd, Romsey, UK
Design: Ken Vail Graphic Design, Cambridge, UK (kvgd.com)
Index by Alison Worthington
Originated by United Graphics, Singapore
Printed in China through Bookbuilders

06 07 08 09 10   10 9 8 7 6 5 4 3 2 1

A CIP catalogue record for this book is available from the British Library.

FOR A CATALOGUE OF ALL BOOKS PUBLISHED BY OSPREY MILITARY AND AVIATION
PLEASE CONTACT:

NORTH AMERICA
Osprey Direct, C/o Random House Distribution Center, 400 Hahn Road, Westminster,
MD 21157
E-mail: info@ospreydirect.com

ALL OTHER REGIONS
Osprey Direct UK, P.O. Box 140, Wellingborough, Northants, NN8 2FA, UK
E-mail: info@ospreydirect.co.uk

www.ospreypublishing.com

Artist's note

Readers may care to note that the original paintings from which
the colour plates in this book were prepared are available for
private sale. All reproduction copyright whatsoever is retained by
the Publishers. All enquiries should be addressed to:

Peter Dennis, The Park, Mansfield, Notts, NG18 2AT, UK

The Publishers regret that they can enter into no correspondence
upon this matter.

Dedication

To my grandmother Irina Nossova.

Acknowledgement

The author wishes to express sincere thanks to Vladimir V.
Golubev who created all the black and white illustrations for this
book.

Editor's note

All the photographs in this book are the property of the author.

The Fortress Study Group (FSG)

The object of the FSG is to advance the education of the public in
the study of all aspects of fortifications and their armaments,
especially works constructed to mount or resist artillery. The FSG
holds an annual conference in September over a long weekend
with visits and evening lectures, an annual tour abroad lasting
about eight days, and an annual Members' Day.
The FSG journal FORT is published annually, and its newsletter
Casemate is published three times a year. Membership is
international. For further details, please contact:

The Secretary, c/o 6 Lanark Place, London W9 1BS, UK.

Contents

Introduction

In 1462 the throne of the Principality of Moscow passed to the Great Prince Ivan III (1462–1505). He subjected the independent lands of Novgorod and Tver to his rule, as well as some of the smaller principalities along the Lithuanian border. Thus, Ivan III practically completed the process of uniting Russian lands around Moscow and became de facto sovereign of a national state. The remaining independent territories were annexed by his son Vasily III (Pskov in 1510 and Ryazan in 1517). One of the direct results of unification was the annihilation of the Mongol yoke imposed on Russia by Batu Khan, son of Genghis Khan, as far back as the mid-13th century. Legend has it that in 1480 Ivan III tore down a Khan's charter, which led to a rather comical war where the two opposing armies positioned themselves on opposite banks of the Ugra River for a long time until the Tatar Army retired. The Golden Horde lost what political influence it had in Russia and disintegrated soon afterwards (1502).

The centralization of the Russian state brought about considerable alterations in the defensive strategy of the country in the second half of the 15th century. Fortresses that used to be on the borders of independent states were now so far from external borders that they were not only of no further use but even potentially dangerous as they might become strongpoints for any rebellion by feudal lords. Consequently, such fortresses were neither restored nor rebuilt. They gradually ceased meeting current military requirements and fell into decay. Meanwhile, fortresses situated close to the borders were renovated and reconstructed to counter potential attacks.

During the rule of Ivan III, as well as that of his son Vasily III (1505–33) and grandson Ivan IV (1533–84), Russia waged constant wars, with varying degrees of success, in the west and south. Her main enemies were now Lithuania and

The Fyodorovskaya and Mitropolich'ya Towers of the kremlin of Novgorod the Great. Jutting from the lines of the walls, the towers had numerous loopholes that enabled the defenders to conduct effective flanking fire. Round and rectangular towers coexisted in the kremlin of Novgorod the Great, as in many other kremlins of the period. The walls used to be covered with shingle.

The tower of Bratski Ostrog. This was part of a structure built by Cossacks in 1652 on the river Angara and had four towers. The tower you can see in the picture was transferred to Moscow in 1959 and now is on view in Kolomenskoye Park.

Poland (Rzeczpospolita after the Lublin Union of 1569), the Livonian Order, Sweden and the Tatar hordes of the Crimea, Kazan and Astrakhan.

Lithuania, the Livonian Order, Poland and Sweden had well-organized armies supplied with powerful artillery and experienced in various siege techniques. Therefore, solid masonry fortresses capable of meeting the challenge were built on the borders – in Pskov, Novgorod, Smolensk and Mozhaisk. The fortress of Smolensk was of particular strategic importance. Situated on the way to Moscow, the town could act as a barrier to the capital or serve as a springboard for an enemy advance depending on whose hands it was in.

On her southern borders Russia had the Tatars. Tatar raids on Russia continued up to the beginning of the 17th century. Their tactic was based on making surprise raids, devastating villages or whole districts and swiftly retiring to the steppes. The Tatars' army consisted of light, highly manoeuvrable cavalry; they had neither efficient infantry nor any siege artillery, hence their extremely rare and usually unsuccessful attacks on fortresses. Most often they just blockaded a town or a fortress with a part of their force, leaving the garrison no chance of making a sortie or the local population of hiding themselves behind the fortress walls. Meanwhile the other part of the army raided nearby villages capturing booty and taking away prisoners. That is why Russia's southern borders needed extensive lines of fortifications, even though the individual fortifications were comparatively weak. These defence lines – called the Bereg, the Zasechnaya Cherta and the Belgorodskaya Cherta – offered the possibility of halting the advance of the enemy until the population could be evacuated and the main force, based in border towns, summoned. The defence system of the southern border was effective as a rule and in most cases the Tatars were prevented from penetrating far into the Russian territory. However, the moment Moscow slackened its defences, the Tatars made raids deep into the country – Khan Mehmed-Girey reached Moscow in 1521; in 1571 the Crimean Khan Devlet-Girey even captured most of the capital before being beaten back from the walls of the Kremlin. Therefore aggressive offensive operations were conducted in addition to defensive measures. Under Ivan IV the Russian state expanded with the capture of Kazan (1552) and Astrakhan (1556), and the river Volga, from source to issue, was now in the hands of Moscow.

Ermak's expedition to Siberia (1581–85) launched the colonization of the territory beyond the Urals. The sparse indigenous population of the vast territories of Siberia was backward in both socio-economic and military terms. There were no armies equipped with powerful artillery and capable of laying a regular siege. Therefore, small wooden forts (*ostrog*), fully adequate for the needs of the colonists, were built here.

Between the years 1604 and 1613 Russia suffered a period of anarchy known as the *smoota* (time of troubles) – surviving a number of pretenders, a devastating civil war, a joint Polish and Swedish invasion and a peasant rebellion. The *smoota* was punctuated by a series of sieges, including those of the Troitse-Sergiev Monastery (1608–10) and Smolensk (1609–11), the fall of Novgorod (1610) and a battle for Moscow; the latter was seized by the Poles in 1610 and besieged by the Russian people's volunteer corps under Lapunov (1611) and Pozharsky (1612).

The *smoota* ended in 1613 with the election of Mikhail Romanov to the Russian throne. Mikhail (1613–45) took advantage of the breathing space to carry out a reform of the army. Several regiments of foreign mercenaries were formed from 1618 to 1632; foreigners taught some of the Russian regiments the art of Western warfare. Tsar Fyodor (1676–82) also carried out European-style military reforms, but it was not until Peter the Great (1682–1725) ascended to the Russian throne that the army was completely reorganized, and this extended to the construction and design of fortifications as well.

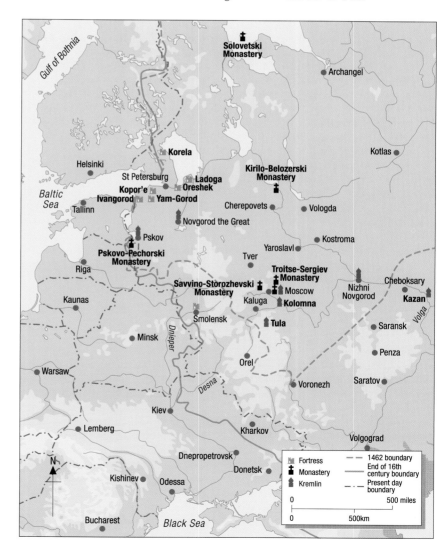

This map shows the location of the kremlins, fortresses and monasteries mentioned in the book.

Chronology

1462	Accession of Great Prince Ivan III to the throne of the Moscow Principality.
1477–78	The annexation of Novgorod by Moscow.
1480	Ivan III refuses to pay tribute to the Tatar Khan. The confrontation on the river Ugra.
1481	The invasion of Livonia by the Russian army.
1492	Foundation of the fortress of Ivangorod.
1492–94	War with Lithuania.
1495–97	War with Sweden.
1495	The siege of Vyborg by Russian troops.
1496	The siege and seizure of Ivangorod by the Swedes.
1500–03	Wars with Lithuania.
1510	The annexation of the Principality of Pskov.
1512–22	Wars with Lithuania and Poland.
1514	The capture of Smolensk by the Russian Army.
1517	The annexation of the Principality of Ryazan.
1521	A massive invasion of Russian territories by the Tatar Army. Khan Mehmed-Girey reaches Moscow. Vasily III agrees to pay tribute.
1547	The first Kazan campaign of Ivan IV.
1549–50	The second Kazan campaign of Ivan IV.
1552	The third Kazan campaign of Ivan IV and the capture of the town.
1556	The seizure of Astrakhan by the Russian Army.
1556–59	The campaigns of Ivan IV against the Crimean Tatars.
1558–83	Wars with Livonia.
1558	The Russian Army lays siege to and takes the fortresses of Narva and Derpt.
1560	The Russian Army seizes the fortresses of Marienburg and Fellin.
1569	Astrakhan attacked by the Turkish Army.
1571	The raid of the Crimean Khan Devlet-Girey on Moscow.
1581	The siege of Pskov by the Polish Army under the command of Stefan Batory.
1581–85	Ermak's Siberian campaign, which marks the beginning of the development of Siberia.
1590–93	War with Sweden.
1604–13	The *smoota* period (time of troubles).
1609–18	Hostilities with Rzeczpospolita.
1609–11	The siege and seizure of Smolensk by the Poles.
1610	The Polish Army takes Moscow and the Kremlin.
1612	The Poles are turned out of Moscow and the Kremlin.
1613–17	War with Sweden.
1615	The siege of Pskov by the Swedish Army under the command of Gustavus Adolphus.
1632–34	War with Rzeczpospolita for the possession of Smolensk.
1637	The Cossacks take Azov, a fortified port belonging to the Crimean Tatars, and offer it to the Russian Tsar; the latter turns down the offer, for fear of a conflict with Turkey, and returns Azov to the Tatars.
1654–67	A war with Rzeczpospolita, which results in Russia's getting part of the Ukraine as well as Kiev and Smolensk.
1654	After a three-month siege the Russian Army takes Smolensk.
1656–58	War with Sweden.
1656	The Russian Army captures the fortresses of Shlisselburg and Nienshanz, but suffers a reverse at the siege of Riga.
1678–81	The Russo-Turkish war for the possession of the Ukraine.
1682	Accession of Peter the Great to the throne of Russia.

The principles of defence

Types of fortifications

The following types of fortifications are characteristic of Russia during the period in question:

Kremlins – fortresses within town walls (citadels). They kept the old name of *detinets* in the territory around Novgorod while were more often called *krom* in the region around Pskov.

Town defensive walls – defensive walls which surrounded settlements populated by craftsmen and traders in towns (*possad*). At the beginning of the period under consideration these fortifications were rather weak as compared with the fortifications of kremlins. However, in the 17th century a kremlin became practically no more than a symbol of a town and lost its defensive significance. The main role in the defence of the towns was now played by outward-looking fortifications.

Defensive walls of monasteries – In the 15th and 16th centuries rich monasteries were fortified with powerful and up-to-date defensive walls, but in the second half of the 17th century these walls lose their strategic importance and become purely decorative.

Fortresses (*krepost'*) and forts (*ostrog*) of purely military significance with a permanent garrison – These were built along the borders of the state as well as in recently annexed territories.

Linear defensive systems – These protected the southern borders from Tatar raids.

The evolution of urban fortifications

Several stages in the development of urban fortifications can be identified. At the beginning of the period most towns only had one fortification – a *detinets* (kremlin), usually situated on a cape at the confluence of two rivers – this is known as a 'cape layout'. Over the course of time towns increased in size and the *detinets* found itself surrounded by a settlement known as the *possad* (the Moscow *possad* later became known as Kitai-Gorod). For protection this settlement was enclosed by a fence, which generally consisted of a continuous chain of palisades – this double layer of fortifications is known as a 'complex cape layout' and was typical of a great number of Russian towns from the 11th to 17th centuries. When the settlement expanded beyond the confines of the cape the resultant layout was known as a 'complex layout'.

Further expansion of a *possad* led to the cultivation of the opposite bank of the rivers. Generally the settlement first spread to the opposite bank of the smaller river (the Neglinnaya River in the case of Moscow). From the 15th century onwards in larger centres these settlements began to be encircled by fortress walls (in Moscow this happened in 1586–93 and the area was called Bely-Gorod). The newly protected area of the town is known as the *blizhneye zarech'e*. Many a large centre such as Pskov or Nizhni Novgorod came to a halt at this stage of their development.

In larger centres a settlement would emerge on the other side of the wider river (the Moskva River in the case of Moscow). In 1591–92 this Moscow *possad* was also enclosed by defensive walls which received the name of Skorodom, later known as Zemlyanoi-Gorod (earth town). These defensive walls encircled the entire territory of Moscow, protecting the settlements on both sides of the river. Such a style of layout is known as *dal'neye zarech'e*. Thus, by the 17th century Moscow found itself defended by four lines of fortifications – the Kremlin, Kitai-Gorod, Bely-Gorod and Zemlyanoi-Gorod. Not every town would go through each stage of the evolutionary process. Some stopped at the stage of 'complex layout', others reached *blizhneye zarech'e*. Moscow was the only city to reach the final stage.

Monasteries

Monasteries played an important part in the defence of a great number of towns. From the second half of the 14th century there was a large increase in the construction of monasteries, usually built on vacant sites outside a town. In the 15th and 16th centuries large cities found themselves surrounded by numerous monasteries, which assumed the function of outposts on the approaches to the town. As a rule, no sooner was a monastery founded than it was enclosed with defensive walls. First, a palisade was built, and then wooden log walls replaced it. Later on, in the 16th and 17th centuries, a monastery of great strategic importance received stone walls. A gate, which was both the main entrance to and the public face of a monastery, was the principal element of its defensive walls. That is why the gate was usually constructed of masonry even if the walls were made of wood. After the church, the bell-tower was the second important element of each monastery. Not only did it notify the inhabitants of the monastery of an enemy's approach, but also passed the news of imminent danger on down the line to the town.

Monasteries could also prove a hindrance to urban defence, as potential besiegers could use them for encampments. So the defenders sometimes preferred to burn them down. For example, Novgorod the Great was surrounded by as many as three concentric lines of monasteries: the first one at a distance of 2–3km from the town fortifications, the second at 5–6km, and the third at 10–12km. However, these monasteries were small and poorly fortified and could not withstand a siege, so the citizens usually destroyed them in the face of an enemy approach. In 1478 they had no time to do this and the monasteries were seized by the Russian troops of Ivan III; hence the fall of the town after a two-month siege and its annexation to the Russian state. Monasteries located on the approaches to Moscow and Pskov were much more strongly fortified and played a significant part in the defence of those cities.

The Novodevichi Nunnery, Moscow. Founded in 1524, this was one of the links in the defensive belt of monasteries on the approaches to Moscow. In the course of its history it was besieged first by the Tatars of the Crimea, then by Polish and Lithuanian forces. The defensive walls of the nunnery were originally made of wood, later replaced by stone, and finally, in the 1680s, rebuilt in brick. By that time the nunnery had lost its military significance and the azure 'crowns' with large windows on top of the towers are vivid evidence of this.

Ladoga Fortress.

This fortress is first mentioned in the year AD 862. It was originally made of wood but by 1114 (possibly earlier) it was rebuilt in stone, becoming the first stone fortress in north Russia. In the 1490s it was rebuilt to meet the requirements of gunpowder artillery (above) and was provided with formidable walls and towers with loopholes to mount cannon in. It is the fortifications of this period that survive to this day; however, only two towers have been preserved, the other three lie in ruin. In 1585–86, three timber-and-earth bastions were added to the stone fortress on the southern side (below). These fortifications consisted of a rampart with a wooden wall made of logs running along the top of it; the wall had three towers. It is probably the earliest Russian fortification to incorporate bastions. (This drawing was based on the reconstruction by E. G. Arapova and A. N. Kirpichnikov.)

Changes in fortification necessitated by the evolution of artillery

In the 15th century fortification development was increasingly influenced by the development of gunpowder artillery. At first artillery was mainly used in the defence, so as early as the beginning of the 15th century fortress towers were being rebuilt so as to be better suited for the installation of artillery. The gate-tower (*nadvratnaya bashnya*) was usually provided with a howitzer-style cannon (*tyufyak*) firing case shot, and the other towers housed ball-firing cannon. Cannon were not yet placed on the walls at this point. The growing part played by artillery led to an increase in the number of towers, especially on the most vulnerable mainland side of fortifications.

By the mid-15th century gunpowder artillery took over from siege machinery as the main weapon of the besieger. Up to the 1470s the defences of stone fortresses were, on the whole, stronger than the weapons of those in attack. Before long, however, the destructive power of gunpowder artillery had grown to such an extent that masonry walls could be breached not only by the balls from gigantic bombards, but also by the fire of a battery of ordinary siege cannon as well. Moreover, as the range of artillery fire had increased considerably, it became possible to bombard a fortress from the other side of a river or ravine, thus depriving the defenders of any topographical advantages. The once-beloved position of a fortress on a cape at the confluence of two rivers or deep ravines, with two out of three sides of the fortress secured by natural obstacles, no longer guaranteed effective protection. While in the past, towers were only erected on the mainland side, now they had to be built all along the perimeter of a fortress and cannon had to be placed in them.

The increasing prevalence of gunpowder artillery also led to a dramatic increase in the use of brick and masonry as a building material from the end of the 15th century onwards. Up to this point only the Moscow Kremlin and the large fortresses around Novgorod and Pskov were built in this way.

'Regular' fortresses

The need to adjust fortifications to the mounting of artillery and to defend them from enemy cannon gave rise to a new style of fortress layout – the so-called 'regular' fortress. These fortresses were of regular geometrical form

Diagram showing the organization of artillery positions in 'regular' fortresses of the 15th and 16th centuries. A 'regular' fortress had straight sections of walls between the towers, which allowed for both frontal and flanking fire. This increased firepower helped the besieged to effectively destroy the attackers at the base of the walls.

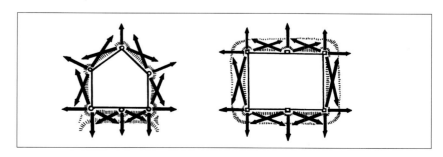

Lagoda Fortress

(triangular, rectangular, trapezoidal or pentagonal) with towers all along the perimeter and straight curtains (*pryasla*); this allowed the defenders to conduct flanking fire from neighbouring towers. The first fortresses of this layout appeared in 1462 in the area around Pskov, and the ideal type of 'regular' fortress is exemplified in the fortress of Ivangorod, built in 1492. It was not always possible due to geographical reasons to give a fortress an absolutely 'regular' layout, and the terrain occasionally dictated that the layout be freer than was ideal. It was also difficult to impose a regular style on older fortresses, so these had their curtain walls straightened and flanking towers added.

Bastioned fortresses

Opinions differ as to when bastioned fortresses were introduced in Russia. Bastions first appeared in Italy at the beginning of the 16th century and quickly spread throughout Europe. The exact time of their emergence in Russia is as yet unknown. There is not a single proof of the existence of bastioned fortresses in Russia until the second half of the 16th century, though it is well known that in the first half of the 16th century towers were encircled by earthwork fortifications but these probably did not have the pentagonal form characteristic of bastions. Most probably, these ramparts were semicircular or rectangular and were designed for two purposes: to protect the foot of the tower against enemy artillery fire and to hold an additional number of cannon, thus increasing the firepower of the tower.

The earliest probable appearance of a bastion dates from 1585–86. At that time timber-and-earth fortifications sized about 170 × 170m were added to the southern side of the Ladoga Fortress. Archaeological excavations have revealed these fortifications consisted of earthen ramparts formed into three bastions. Stretching along the top of the rampart was a wooden log wall with three hexagonal towers, – two on the bastion projections and one (the gate-tower) on the curtain itself. It was generally typical of the early bastion systems in Russia to have a wooden log wall or even a tower located on top of a bastion or a curtain. Later on such superstructures were discarded.

Bastions become a common feature of fortifications in Russia from the late 16th century onwards. Novgorod the Great and Rostov the Great strengthened their fortifications with bastions in 1631–33, while Zemlyanoi-Gorod in Moscow received its nine bastions at the end of the 1630s. A great number of other fortresses were fortified with bastions throughout the course of the 17th century.

Monasteries on the other hand, even those built in the second half of the 17th century, were still surrounded with the same style of fortress walls common in the 15th and 16th centuries. Monks were sometimes known to oppose the erection of earthen fortifications for reasons of piety as they did not consider earthwork defences to be elegant enough for a holy site. For example, in 1653 the Kirilo-Belozerski Monastery was to be encircled by earthwork fortifications with bastions, but the monks revolted and even appealed to the Tsar, begging him to permit them to build ordinary stone walls. Most monasteries' walls became purely decorative in the 17th century, hence numerous decorations on the walls and towers of the monasteries dating from this period.

The original view of Ivangorod Fortress, 1492. Initially this fortress was built as an ideal 'regular' fortress. However, the towers did not protrude beyond the line of the walls far enough and the besieged could not conduct efficient flanking fire. As a result, as early as 1496 the Swedes captured the fortress. In the same year the Russians took it back and completely rebuilt it, which took just 12 weeks.

Design and development

All fortresses consisted of three main elements: walls, towers and gates. In most fortresses (except the most primitive or those well protected by natural defences) there was also a ditch in front of the walls. However, the structure and material of each of these three elements depended to a great extent on the significance attached to the fortress. Walls of brick or masonry were only given to fortresses of great strategic importance, as well as to kremlins and urban fortifications of major cities. Fortresses of minor military significance had wooden walls of log construction. In small forts (*ostrog*) a palisade (*tyn*) often served as a wall. Such forts were usually constructed on a rectangular layout with towers on each corner and one gate in the gate-tower. *Ostrogs* were more widely spread in Siberia and on the extremes of the state.

Walls

In the late 15th century, as a consequence of the increased power of gunpowder artillery, the walls of Russian fortresses went through considerable changes. Historically, these walls had narrowed slightly to the top and been flat on both sides, they now acquired both a talus (thickening of the lower part of the wall) and a *prikladka* (a masonry reinforcement on the external side). The talus sometimes reached as far as halfway up the wall and was principally designed to weaken the impact of cannon fire, as the shot caused less damage to a sloping surface.

Beginning in the late 15th century loopholes and embrasures became widespread at the very bottom of walls (*podoshvenny boy*). These were mainly designed for the installation of artillery, though they could also be used for shooting handguns. In order to install a cannon, a chamber (*pechura*) was made inside the wall reinforced by compass arches. These arches ran the whole length of the wall, not just the parts with embrasures. On the whole, blind arches were more numerous than those with embrasures. Such walls with arches first appeared in the Moscow Kremlin during its reconstruction in 1485–95 before spreading to other Russian fortresses.

Loopholes or embrasures situated halfway up the wall (*sredni boy*) were also used, but far less often than *podoshvenny boy*. So that the strength and integrity of the wall was not undermined, *podoshvenny* and *sredni boys* were arranged in a chessboard pattern. A wall of this construction was first built in Smolensk in

The walls of Smolensk, 1596. The three-tiered fighting structure seen in these walls was the first structure of this kind in Russia. There were galleries with loopholes on three levels: lower, middle and upper (with a parapet). The loopholes were set in a chessboard pattern so as to both cover dead ground and avoid weakening the walls.

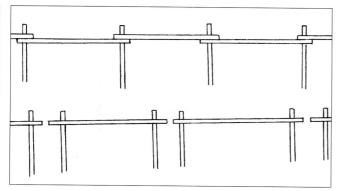

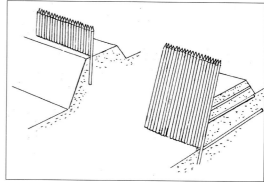

the late 16th century where the *pechuras* of a *sredni boy* were located at a height of 5m above the ground, accessible via ladders.

Stone walls, as well as wooden ones, were crowned with a wall-walk (*boevoy hod*) covered with a wooden roof. By the late 15th century, due to Italian influence, the merlons of many walls (especially kremlins') were given the shape of a swallow's tail and provided with loopholes. It is sometimes mistakenly believed that the saddles of such 'two-horned' merlons served as mounts for handguns. However, their height completely rules this out. For example, the merlons of the Tula Kremlin are 2.5m high.

From the second half of the 15th century wooden log walls built in the *tarassy* style began to replace those built in the earlier *gorodni* style. In the *gorodni* style the wall was built of separate log cells placed next to each other (the individual cells were called *gorodni*) but not joined together. Because of the gaps between these log cells the wall lacked strength. In the *tarassy* style, the wall was constructed of overlapping longitudinal logs strengthened with single cross-wise walls every 6 to 8m. As a result, the wall was constructed of a continuous joined chain of log cells. The individual cells were called *tarassy* and they could be of rectangular, trapezoidal or triangular form. Some of the cells were filled with earth or stones and some were left empty and open on the inside in order that cannon could be placed there.

It is probable that the *tarassy* style appeared much earlier than the 15th century (one comes across intrarampart log frameworks of this construction dating as far back as the 12th century) but it did not become common before the mid-15th century. It is likely that the mass adoption of this style was provoked by the growing power of gunpowder artillery, as wooden log cells filled with earth protected against cannon fire at least as well as, and sometimes even better than, masonry structures. Moreover, a breach in a wooden wall with an earth filling caused much less destruction than the equivalent breach in a stone wall. The construction of wooden walls was also much cheaper than of stone ones and took less time; and timber, unlike stone, was always easily available in Russia.

Stretching along the top of a wooden wall was a *boevoy hod*, divided by small cross-wise walls into separate sections. The parapet usually projected a little bit out over the main wall creating a kind of a machicolation, which was known as an *oblam* in Russia. All this wooden structure running along the top of the wall – the wall-walk, the parapet with loopholes and the roof – made up the *zaborola*. This structure tended to be the first target of any besieger.

Tarassy-style fortifications

A wooden log wall built in the *tarassy* style. This was a style of building in wood common in Russia in the 15th and 16th centuries. *Tarassy* were wooden cells joined together by overlapping longitudinal logs. The cells could be rectangular, trapezoidal or triangular in shape. The *tarassy* were often filled up with earth or small stones. Wooden walls of this type could withstand artillery fire as well as those made of stone. This plate also shows an intra-rampart wooden structure.

Tarrasy-style fortifications

In the more important fortresses *tarassy* walls were sometimes constructed of two rows of framework. At the same time, in smaller forts *(ostrog)*, walls could be quite simple – just a palisade *(tyn)* or a row of logs laid horizontally and fixed between vertical poles dug into the ground. A *tyn* in an *ostrog* could be placed vertically (such a palisade was called *stoyachi ostrog*) or obliquely, inclined in the direction of the interior of the fort *(kosoi ostrog)*.

Ditches

Ditches in Russia, even as late as the 16th and 17th centuries, consisted of nothing but earth and were very rarely faced with stone (the Moscow Kremlin is one of the exceptions). The ditch was generally dug out at between 2 and 14m from the wall (this distance is known as the berm), the higher the wall the further the ditch was from it. This distance was needed both to prevent the wall sliding into the ditch and also to allow the defenders to command the whole ditch despite the lack of machicolation on the walls. Once machicolations *(varovy boy)* began to be installed on walls, the distance between the wall and the ditch lost its importance.

Different types of rectangular towers seen in Siberian *ostrogs*. Most wooden towers were rectangular and had three to four storeys. The upper storey projected over the lower ones, creating an overhang (*oblam*) that allowed the defenders to drop objects onto and shoot at the attackers below. These towers were often crowned with a watch tower.

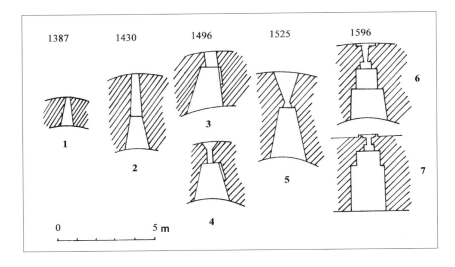

The evolution of loophole design. These loopholes are shown in cross-section:
1 – the small tower of Porkhov;
2 – the middle tower of Porkhov;
3, 4 – the gate-tower of Ivangorod;
5 – the Gremyach'ya Tower of Pskov;
6, 7 – *pryasla* (walls) of Smolensk.

Towers

Wooden towers of Russian fortresses could be rectangular or polygonal. The latter were less common; they were usually much bigger than rectangular ones. Polygonal towers were often used as gatehouses; they were also built in fortresses of a complicated layout as they allowed walls to be joined at angles other than 90 degrees. Local preferences also left their mark on the popularity of this or that type of tower. Thus, they were especially fond of polygonal towers in the Russian north: in Olonets there were ten hexagonal towers for three rectangular ones, while in Holmogory seven towers out of 11 were hexagonal.

On top of the towers there was a small projection (about 15–25cm) known as an *oblam*, which served the same purpose as a machicolation. As a rule, a tower had either square or rectangular loopholes on each floor, small (8–10cm) for handguns and larger (30–40cm) for cannon.

Masonry towers came in three types: rectangular, circular and polygonal. Polygonal towers did not appear in Russian fortresses until the end of the 15th century and are often confused with the earlier, 'circular' style in documents.

Loopholes inside the Namestnik (vicegerent) Tower of Ivangorod Fortress. Note the flue in the centre between the embrasures.

17

The Tainichnaya Tower of the kremlin in Nizhni Novgorod. As seen from the name, there was a *tainik* in the tower. Each storey was provided with firing positions (*pechuras*) for cannon, and each embrasure had a flue to remove the smoke.

RIGHT **The Dmitrovskaya Gate-tower of Nizhni Novgorod Kremlin.**

This gate is a typical example of a complex gate of the period and consists of a gate-tower (the Dmitrovskaya Tower, 1) protected by a low tower open on the top and the inside (an *otvodnaya strel'nitsa*, 2) and a fortified bridge (3) across a moat. The *otvodnaya strel'nitsa* is connected with the bank of the moat by another bridge. Drawbridges protect the gates of both the Dmitrovskaya Tower and the *otvodnaya strel'nitsa*. An enemy wishing to make his way into the kremlin by this gate would have to first capture the *otvodnaya strel'nitsa*, then the fortified bridge, get across the gap between the bridge and the Dmitrovskaya Tower, and finally, force his way through the gate of the tower. (This drawing is based on the reconstruction by S. L. Agafonov.)

Circular and rectangular towers often co-existed in the same fortress, indeed fortresses with only one type of tower (either circular or rectangular) are quite unusual. There does not seem to have been any set rules as to the arrangement of particular types of tower around the perimeter of the fortress, though circular towers were more often put on the corners of a fortress with square ones in the middle of a fortress wall; the gate-tower (*nadvratnaya bashnya*) was always rectangular.

Stone towers were supplied with numerous firing positions which could be used for handguns as well as cannon. These chambers had funnel-shaped openings pointing outwards, which made it easier to position cannon barrels. They were sometimes built with flues, but more often flues were built outside the chamber and many fortresses had no flues at all. Firing positions were made wide enough for the barrel of the cannon to protrude outside and this partly made up for the absence of flues.

From the late 15th century onwards a large number of stone towers were built with a talus in a similar style to that becoming common on fortress walls. Communication between the different floors of a tower was realized either with

The Pskovo-Pechorski Nunnery. Note the shape of the loopholes, there are also box machicolations overhanging the gate (to the right of the tower). The gate itself is concealed by earthworks.

The Dmitrovskaya Gate-tower of Nizhni Novgorod Kremlin

A cutaway view of stone (left and centre) and wooden towers from the 16th–17th centuries. Most stone and wooden towers had three to four storeys and pitched roofs. The role of machicolation in stone towers was undertaken by a projection of the upper storey (*oblam*) in wooden towers.

the help of wooden ladders and hatches, or steps cut in the thick stone walls. On the upper floor of the tower there was a parapet with merlons, which often projected beyond the surface of the wall, forming a machicolation (*varovy boy*). Box machicolations were never popular in Russia, although from time to time they appear in fortifications of the 16th century. As an alternative to machicolations, loopholes were sunk directly into the thick wall of a tower with wide funnel-shaped openings directed downwards. Like machicolations, they allowed the besieged to control the area at the foot of the wall or tower.

Both masonry and wooden towers were covered with pitched wooden roofs, sometimes provided with an observation point on top fenced with a balustrade, which, in its turn, was covered with a smaller pitched roof.

Communication between towers and the wall-walk (*boevoy hod*) was realized in one of the following two ways: either the wall-walk went through the tower – in this case the tower had an exit to the wall on either side – or the tower had only one exit, to the rear, which led to a special platform connected with the wall-walk. The first style was characteristic of towers situated along the length of the wall while the second type was typical of corner towers. In the fortress of Ivangorod a gap covered by a drawbridge was left between the tower and the wall-walk, though this is unique in Russia for the period and may well have been influenced by foreign designs.

Towards the end of the 15th century a *tainik* – a tunnel leading to a well – was often located in the tower nearest to the river. That is why one can come across a tower called a *tainichnaya bashnya* (from *tainik*) in almost all the fortresses of the period.

Gates

Fortress gates of the 16th and 17th centuries were not located in a curtain between two towers but in a tower itself (the *nadvratnaya bashnya*). The gateway was usually provided with two leaves (external and internal). As often as not it curved at right angles, so that the enemy had to take a turn to get from one gate to the other. This made siege techniques useless as a means of breaking the second gate. Movable gratings (portcullises), which appeared in Russia as far back as the 14th century, were commonplace.

Gates could be situated in two ways. In the first instance the gate was built into the side of a tower, so when approaching the gate, a potential enemy had to move along the fortress wall with his unprotected right-hand side exposed to fire.

In the other case the gate was built at the front of a tower, but the approaches to it were commanded from a second gate-tower, the *otvodnaya strel'nitsa*. This tower was lower than the main gate-tower and usually

The gate and the loophole protecting the entrance of the Ladoga Fortress. The gate leading into the Ladoga Fortress is in the tower and is curved at 90 degrees while the gate arch itself was placed on the side of the tower; as a result, the enemy, when approaching the gate, had to proceed along the right side of the wall right under the defenders' fire. This was the most common type of gateway in Russian fortresses of the period.

situated across a moat, connected to the main gate-tower by a permanent bridge or drawbridge.

Drawbridges appeared in Russia in the late 15th century. They were built in such a way that, when drawn up, they barred the passage. Sometimes the bridge across the moat was a permanent one, made of stone, in which case a long fortified gallery was built across it. The Troitskie Gate of the Moscow Kremlin was protected by an *otvodnaya strel'nitsa* and a fortified bridge. In order to get into a fortress through a gate the besiegers had to break through the *otvodnaya strel'nitsa*, cross the moat, and fight through a gate and the portcullis in the main gate-tower of the fortress whilst under fire from the fortification.

These two types of complex gates were only built in fortresses of major military significance. In minor fortresses a gate could be of the simplest design – in the facade of a tower with a through gateway and a simple wooden bridge on supports.

Different types of gate-towers as seen in Siberian *ostrogs*. Gate-towers could be rectangular or multangular. A small chapel was often found over a gate, as seen on the two left-hand towers.

A small chapel built in a balcony above the gateway was characteristic of a Russian *nadvratnaya bashnya*. One could enter the chapel from the first storey of the tower. These chapels were of purely religious significance and softened the severe look of the towers. The tradition of building small chapels above a gateway goes back to the times of the Kievan Rus' and lasted up to the 18th century. In smaller fortresses, such as Siberian *ostrogs,* they were the only chapels in the fortress. An icon was sometimes put over a minor gate instead of a chapel.

Construction

Wooden walls were either the extension of the intrarampart wooden framework or they were put on piles specially driven into the rampart. The first way was more ancient and used from the time of the Kievan Rus'.

As a rule, logs in the framework were joined 'v oblo', with the ends of the logs sticking outwards. The upper log was put into a semicircular groove cut in the lower log. The other layout, with a semicircular groove cut in the upper log, was considered inferior as it caused the logs to rot much quicker. This second method had largely fallen out of use in the period under consideration. With the building of towers, the logs were joined together not only by the 'v oblo' method but also by 'v lapu', where the ends of the logs were specially trimmed so that they did not stick out from the wall. The 'v lapu' method allowed the building of polygonal towers as well as rectangular ones.

The roof over the walls and towers was usually made 'v dva tyossa', with two layers of thin planks overlapping each other so that the upper layer covered the gaps in the lower one. A covering made of one layer of planks was less common as it did not adequately protect against leakage. The ends of the planks usually had the shape of feathers or merlons.

Masonry walls were built on special wooden flooring placed over piles driven into the ground. The masonry was usually semi-rubble, with the wall resembling a sandwich with a core of some other substance between the two outer layers. Up to the late 15th century the outer layers were preferably made of harder sorts of stone, e.g. boulders, which made early cannon balls bounce

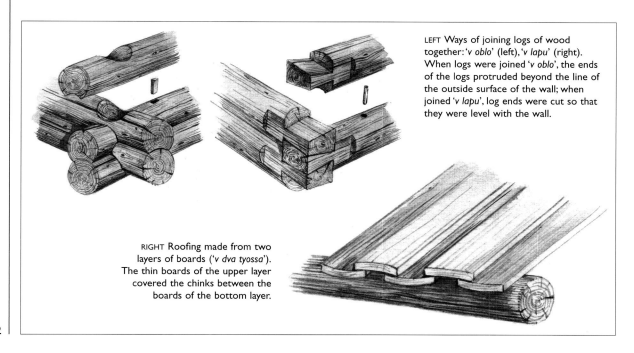

LEFT Ways of joining logs of wood together: 'v oblo' (left), 'v lapu' (right). When logs were joined 'v oblo', the ends of the logs protruded beyond the line of the outside surface of the wall; when joined 'v lapu', log ends were cut so that they were level with the wall.

RIGHT Roofing made from two layers of boards ('v dva tyossa'). The thin boards of the upper layer covered the chinks between the boards of the bottom layer.

back or split. The core of the wall was filled with a layer of crushed stone or soft cobblestones mixed with mortar. By the end of the 15th century, however, the destructive power of gunpowder artillery had grown to such an extent that, when a ball struck a wall, the boulders became loose and fell out. So the external layers of the wall began to be faced with polished flagstones, with a layer of harder stone behind them for added protection against artillery fire. Monolithic construction was much less common than semi-rubble. Stones were never laid dry, but always on mortar.

Additional strength was given to stone walls and towers by the introduction of log ties – longitudinal or traverse logs, sometimes even whole horizontal frames, placed in two or three tiers up the wall. In the 16th and 17th centuries iron structures were often introduced in stone walls instead of wooden ties.

Although typical of the earlier period, beamed ceilings were still used in stone towers of the period, though from the late 15th century most towers were built with vaulted ceilings as well.

From the late 15th century the use of brick in construction became popular. Brick was first used only in military architecture; for instance, the walls of Kitai-Gorod are wholly made of brick. However, masonry and brick were sometimes used together. In this case masonry was used for the lower part of a wall, or as a filling for the core, while brick was used for facing walls or building the upper part of a wall. Both ways were used in Smolensk where the foundation and the lower part of the wall were built from white stone as a protection against mining; the middle section had a rubble core with external brick layers; and the uppermost part consisted of a wholly brick parapet.

In Russia they tended to do masonry work from mid-April, once the ice had melted, till mid-September, when the rainy and cold weather began to set in.

ABOVE LEFT The Vladimirskaya Tower of the kremlin of Novgorod the Great. Note the decorations and the icon over the gate.

ABOVE RIGHT The Spasskaya Tower of the kremlin of Novgorod the Great. On this tower an ornamental band of diamond-shaped sockets and round rosettes can be seen. Such ornaments became very common in the decoration of Russian fortresses from the early 15th century.

Semi-rubble walling of the north-western wall of the kremlin in Nizhni Novgorod. With semi-rubble walling, the wall consisted of three layers: there was a layer of small broken stones mixed with grouting between the two external layers. Semi-rubble walling was the most common type of masonry construction during the period.

Any breaking of this rule could lead to dire consequences. The Smolensk fortifications were erected in 1595–1602 in such a hurry that the work had to be carried on late into the autumn. As a result, part of the defensive wall built at that time proved flimsy, and the Poles, informed by a traitor, took advantage of it during the siege of 1609–11.

Wooden walls and towers were often coated with turf or clay. This not only protected the walls from fire but also gave the fortifications a more impressive appearance. Stone fortifications were never whitewashed until the mid-17th century.

Up to the 16th century builders erected stone fortifications standing on wooden planking set up on transverse wooden beams. These were fixed in the masonry at various levels as the wall grew. On the completion of the work the planking was removed and the beams taken out or cut down. The gaps left from these beams were sometimes filled, but often left as they were and these gaps can be seen in some fortresses to this day. In the 16th century scaffolding began to be used for construction work.

The construction work was carried out by the local people who were instructed to turn up equipped with tools. They worked for a certain length of time and then were replaced with others. The construction of fortifications (*gorodovoye delo*) was one of the hardest duties for the local people. Construction work was in the charge of a *gorodnik* – a military engineer who occupied a sufficiently high social position. A building reform was passed in 1534 introducing a wider than before usage of the population in the construction of fortifications. Soldiers, townsfolk and 'other people, all and sundry', were to be enlisted in case of emergency.

From the start of the 15th century the Russian government began to invite foreign craftsmen to assist in the construction of fortifications much more often than before. Under Ivan III (1462–1505) a number of envoys were sent to Italy with a special mission to engage the services of Italian engineers for construction work in Russia. As a result, in 1475 well-known Italian architects and engineers began to arrive in Moscow. Among them were Rodolfo Fioravanti, Pietro Antonio Solari and others whose names appear in contemporary chronicles followed by the word *fryazin* (foreigner). They erected churches and cathedrals, palaces and chambers and, particularly, fortifications. The first of the major projects carried out by foreign craftsmen was the reconstruction of the Moscow Kremlin in the late 15th century.

The number of newly arrived craftsmen grew with every year. Under Ivan IV (1533–84) there were enough to form a corporation of their own. They were first called masonry wall masters, then fortification master builders (*gorododelets*), and in the 17th century they acquired the honourable rank of engineers. From that time on the corporation was divided into foreign engineers (supervising projects as a rule), master builders (mostly Russians), apprentices and draughtsmen. Besides Italians, master builders from other countries were also engaged. The Scots architect and clockmaker Christopher Galloway took part in the construction of the St Florus Tower (called the Spasskaya) of the Moscow Kremlin, which was completed in 1625.

Tour of the sites

The fortifications of Moscow

The evolution of Russian defensive fortifications can be amply illustrated by the example of the city of Moscow. By the 17th century the defensive lines around Moscow outnumbered those of any other Russian town.

Moscow is first mentioned in the annals of 1147 as a small settlement on the outskirts of the Vladimiro-Suzdal Principality. Like most other towns, Moscow's fortifications were represented by a single small *detinets* (kremlin) located on a hill on the cape at the confluence of the Moskva and Neglinnaya Rivers. In 1156 the *detinets* saw its defensive walls replaced by more solid ones and its territory enlarged. In the course of its long history, the Moscow Kremlin underwent reconstruction and enlargement more than once. The most significant works were those done in 1339–40, when the walls of the Kremlin were built of thick oak logs. After the great fire of 1365 destroyed the Kremlin, its wooden walls were at last replaced with masonry ones.

In due course the masonry walls fell into decay due to numerous sieges and fires. The latter destroyed the wooden ties of the masonry, causing the collapse of the walls. In damaged places, masonry walls were replaced with wooden ones. By the late 15th century little was left of the former beauty and power of the Moscow Kremlin. Meanwhile, the rapid development of gunpowder artillery and the political image of the capital of a newly born centralized Russian state demanded that a new Kremlin be erected. Therefore, in 1485–95 the Moscow Kremlin was completely reconstructed under the supervision of Italian master builders Antonio Jilardi (Anton Fryazin), Marko Ruffo (Mark Fryazin), Pietro Antonio Solari (Petr Fryazin) and Alevisio da Milano (Aleviz), who, quite naturally, introduced their own style into Russian architecture. As a result, the Moscow Kremlin resembles Sforza Castle in Milan. It is the fortifications of this period, with some later modifications, that can be seen to this day.

General view of the Moscow Kremlin from the bridge over the Moskva River. The Kremlin fortifications visible today were built in 1485–95. The parapet of the Moscow Kremlin is crowned with swallow's-tail merlons due to the influence of Italian craftsmen who took part in the building of the Kremlin. In the 17th century the Moscow Kremlin lost its military significance and became a symbol of the centralized Russian state.

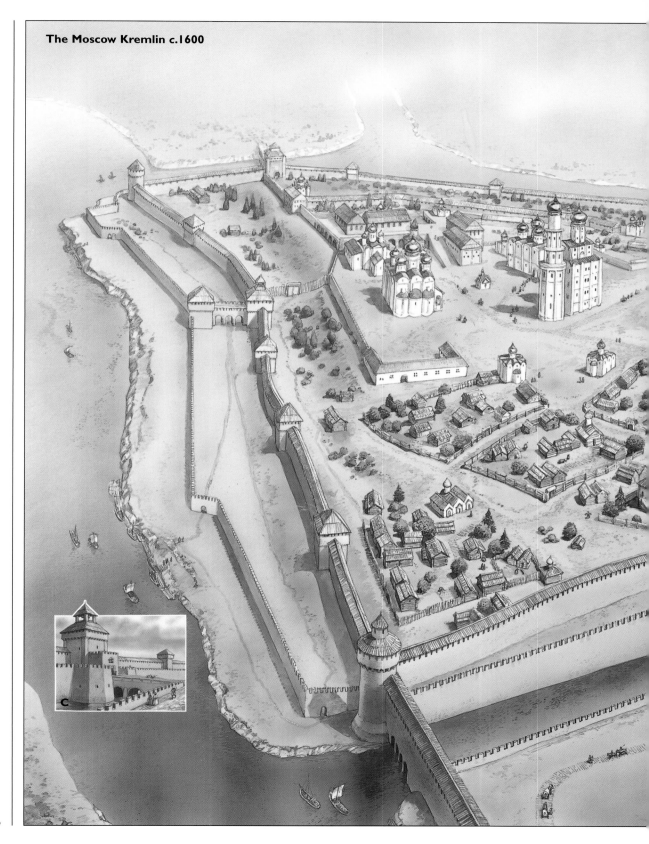

C

B

A

The Moscow Kremlin c.1600

Built in 1485–95 the Moscow Kremlin was improved throughout the course of the 16th century. It was then that it was provided with a moat connecting the two rivers so that it found itself encircled by water on all sides, as well as by low walls on either side of the moat and along the Moskva River. In the inset details you can see fragments of the Moscow Kremlin in close-up: A – the Troitskaya Tower connected to the Kutaf'ya Tower (*otvodnaya strel'nitsa*) by a bridge; B – the Tainitskaya Tower, which derived its name from a secret exit to a well, was also provided with a bridgehead tower (*otvodnaya strel'nitsa*); C – the Spasskaya Tower and a moat fortified by low external walls on either bank. Today the Moscow Kremlin looks quite different – the moat has been filled up (Red Square was laid out on this site), the external walls have been pulled down, all the towers have been built on with decorative superstructures and the wooden roofing on the walls has not survived.

Two fragments of a picture of 1601 showing the Moscow Kremlin. In the left-hand picture is the Spasskaya Tower. On either side of the moat there are low walls, uncharacteristic of Russian fortifications, surmounted by merlons; the main walls have overhangs by the towers and especially the gates. So on this side the Moscow Kremlin is protected by three rings of walls. Today these low walls no longer exist, the moat has been filled up and the site is now Red Square. Shown in the right-hand picture is the Troitskie Gate, which consists of the Troitskaya Gate-tower, connected to the *otvodnaya strel'nitsa* (the Kutaf'ya Tower) by a fortified bridge. The fortifications of this section of the Kremlin were built in 1495 and were the first example of bridgehead fortifications (*otvodnaya strel'nitsa*) in Russia.

The Troitskie Gate of the Moscow Kremlin. This gate is a typical example of a complex gate of the period and consists of a gate-tower (the Troitskaya Tower) protected by an *otvodnaya strel'nitsa* (the Kutaf'ya Tower) and a fortified bridge across a moat. Historically, the bridge did not reach the tower – a drawbridge joined it to the Troitskaya Tower and a sliding floor to the Kutaf'ya Tower. An enemy wishing to make his way into the Kremlin would have to first capture the *otvodnaya strel'nitsa* (the Kutaf'ya Tower), climb onto the bridge and take possession of it, then get across a precipice between the bridge and the Troitskaya Tower, and, finally, force his way through the gate of the tower. The decor of large windows and semi-columns on top of the Kutaf'ya Tower was added later, when the tower had lost its defensive role.

The Moscow Kremlin was built of brick though the old masonry walls, wherever they were well preserved, were not dismantled but just faced with brick. All in all, the walls of the Kremlin stretched for 2,235m. Depending on the section, the walls were 9–13m high (merlons including) and 3.5–6.5m thick. Running along the top of the wall was a wall-walk 2.2–3.8m wide protected by 2–2.5m-high merlons; it used to be covered with a wooden double-pitched roof (which burned down in 1737). The merlons have the form of a swallow's tail (due to the Italian influence) and have loopholes. Arches were built on the inner side of the wall with a *podoshvenny boy* in some of them and *sredni boy* added to the most vulnerable curtains. Eighteen towers providing flanking fire were evenly distributed along the walls at a greatest distance apart of 200m. The towers had three to five combat tiers and had both loopholes and machicolations. Two corner towers were circular, one polyhedral and all the rest square. There were six gate-towers. They had either drawbridges or easily removable bridges in front of them and portcullises inside them. Moreover, three of the gates were protected on the outside by separately

standing towers (*otvodnaya strel'nitsa*). It was the first time that bridgehead fortifications were used in Russia. Only one of such towers survives, the Kutaf'ya Tower. It used to be connected with the Troitskaya Tower by a bridge that did not come close to either of the towers, being connected to them by drawbridges. It seems that the other gate-towers had a similar structure. Underground passages (*sluh*), intended for detecting enemy sapper works, led outside the Kremlin's walls.

The Moscow Kremlin was additionally fortified in 1508–16. A moat 36m wide and 8–16m deep was dug on its eastern side, where Red Square is today. The sides of the moat were faced with masonry and brick. Thus the Kremlin found itself protected by water on all sides: by the rivers (Moskva and Neglinnaya) on two sides and by the moat on the third. Towards the end of the 16th century fairly low brick walls with swallow's-tail merlons were built on either side of the moat as well as on the side of the Moskva River.

It's interesting to note that the Moscow Kremlin was not always red brick, i.e. it did not always look the colour the tourists see today. Originally, the brick-built Kremlin of the 15th century was red, but later it was whitewashed all over. The first reliable evidence of it being whitewashed goes back to 1680, but some parts of it might have been whitewashed earlier. Then, up to the 20th century it was white, and only in the Soviet period was the whitewash removed and the Kremlin coated with a special red paint to make it look like brick.

Adjacent to the Kremlin was the great *possad* (trading quarter), known as the Kitai-Gorod since the 16th century, it was first fortified in 1394. At that time the fortifications comprised a rampart and a palisade with a ditch in front of it. In 1534–38 Kitai-Gorod was encircled by a solid brick wall with thickset towers. The Kitai-Gorod wall stretched from the Arsenal'naya Tower to the Beklemishevskaya Tower of the Moscow Kremlin, a distance of 2.6km. Although it was not very high (6.5–9m), it was, however, extraordinarily thick – over 6m. Its thickness allowed a 4m-wide wall-walk to be made, which enabled a two-horse team to quickly pull cannon onto the wall. Artillery was mounted here in both the towers and inside the walls themselves, at both upper and lower levels. Thus, the wall of Kitai-Gorod made it possible for artillery fire to be brought to bear from two wall layers as well as from the towers, providing for greater firepower. The walls were crowned with rectangular merlons, each with three loopholes: the central one for cannon and the two on either side for handguns. The walls also had machicolations to bring fire to bear on the approaches to the walls. During times of peace the loopholes were covered with wooden shutters and the embrasures for the *podoshvenny boy* were blocked with brick. Fourteen low-built solid towers were located along the walls. They were circular, polygonal or rectangular in shape. The towers were splayed out, with the talus reaching as far as half the height of the tower. Special rooms were built under the towers with copper sheets hanging on the walls. These were called *sluhs* (sing. *sluh*) and allowed the defenders to detect and locate the direction in which the enemy was digging a mine gallery. The red-brick walls of Kitai-Gorod matched the Kremlin walls and surviving evidence shows that foreigners considered them as one unit, which they called Krasny Gorod (red fortress). In the second half of the 17th century the walls of Kitai-Gorod were painted white, though they were later returned to their original red colour which they bear to this day.

The expanded *possad* needed protection and the years 1586–93 saw the erection of a new fortress wall covering the suburbs of Kitai-Gorod and the *possad* on the other bank of the Neglinnaya River. This wall, called the Bely-Gorod, joined the Kremlin on one side and the walls of Kitai-Gorod on the other. With 7,000 masons engaged in the construction process, the fortifications were assembled very quickly. The vertical walls (without a talus at the foot) were 10m high and 4.5m thick. The *boevoy hod* on the top was protected by swallow's-tail merlons, some of which had loopholes, while others

The walls of Kitai-Gorod were built in 1534–38 to protect the outer extent of the Moscow Kremlin. They are made of solid brick without any filling and are fortified with low towers.

were left blind. Traditional arches were to be found on the inner side, some of them supplied with *pechuras* and *podoshvenny boy*. Twenty-seven towers (13–20m high) were situated at irregular intervals around the perimeter, at a distance varying from 220 to 610m (339m on average). The towers and the walls were covered with wooden roofs. The part of the wall that crossed the Neglinnaya River had an arch closed with a portcullis. On the whole, the walls of Bely-Gorod were already obsolete by the time of their erection and were defensively inferior to the walls of Kitai-Gorod built half a century before.

The walls of Bely-Gorod were over 9.5km long and enclosed more than 512ha. Even so, by the time of their erection, the fortifications left a considerable part of the populated territory unprotected. In 1591 the Crimean Tatars, led by Khan Kazy-Girei, raided Moscow. The Tatars were put to flight by artillery fire but in their retreat they burned down the unprotected suburbs. In the face of potential further Tatar raids, measures were taken to fortify the unprotected *possads*, including the one across the Moskva River. By 1592 a new ring of defensive walls encircled Moscow. The fortifications of this new defensive ring comprised a ditch about 16m wide and an earthen rampart with a wooden wall on top. Made from oak logs, the wall was 6 x 6m. Fifty-seven towers were erected along the perimeter, out of which 12 were gate-towers. Only two gate-towers were masonry, all the others were made of wood. The gate-towers had a rectangular form and the rest were polygonal. The gate-towers were equipped with six cannon each, while the others had four cannon. The fortifications in total were about 15km long and were known as the Derevyanny-Gorod (wooden fortifications) though more colloquially they were called Skorodom (quickly built habitation). Polish invaders burnt down the wooden walls of Skorodom in 1611, and in the late 1630s the rampart was restored with nine bastions added to the southern side. Since that time the fortifications have been known as Zemlyanoi-Gorod (earth fortifications). The same name was given to the territory encircled by the walls. Wooden log walls were once more added to the rampart in 1659.

The centre of Moscow, as well as its suburbs, was additionally protected by monasteries. The first group, namely the Alekseevski, Krestovozdvizhenski, Nikitski, Georgiyevski, Varsonovievski, Zlatoustovski and Ivanovski monasteries, comprised the monasteries in the central part of the city. They were situated at an equal distance from each other and flanked the centre of

The fortifications of Moscow in the 17th century

At that time the fortifications of Moscow included the Kremlin, Kitai-Gorod, Bely-Gorod, and Skorodom (later known as Zemlyanoi-Gorod). The fortifications of the latter enclosed the Moscow *possads* (suburban settlements) on both sides of the river in a ring. Such a layout is conventionally called *dal'neye zarech'e*. On this plan one can also see the monasteries that protected the centre of Moscow as well as its suburbs. Insets show reconstructed fragments of the fortifications of Kitai-Gorod (A), Bely-Gorod (B), and Skorodom (C).

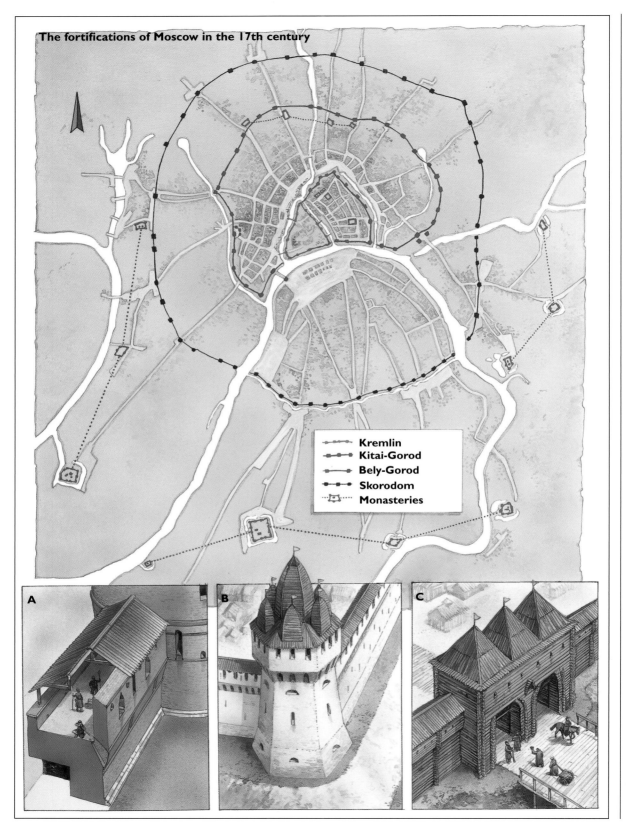

The fortifications of Moscow in the 17th century

Kremlin
Kitai-Gorod
Bely-Gorod
Skorodom
Monasteries

A

B

C

Moscow to the north, west and east. The second group, consisting of 14 monasteries, were situated further from the centre. Four monasteries – Strastnoy, Vysoko-Petrovski, Rozhdestvenski and Sretenski – protected the city to the north. Four monasteries commanded the most vulnerable southern approaches – Simonov, Danilovski, Donskoi and Andreevski. The western approaches were covered by three monasteries: Novodevichi, Savvin and Novinski. The same number of monasteries is found in the east – Spaso-Andronnikov, Pokrovski and Novospasski. They commanded the Vladimirskaya and Ryazanskaya roads as well as the Yauza River.

Nizhni Novgorod Kremlin

The kremlin that can be seen today was built at the beginning of the 16th century, right after the reconstruction of the Moscow and Novgorod kremlins. The walls are 1,802m long and built of white stone and red brick. On average the walls are 9–10.5m high and 4.5–5.0m thick. The external side has a slight slope (up to 8 degrees) which is separated from the vertical upper part by a small decorative ledge. The internal side is perfectly vertical and supplied with arches. Imitating the Moscow Kremlin, the walls were crowned with swallow's-tail merlons. The lack of *sredni* or *podoshvenny boy* loopholes is a distinctive feature of the Nizhni Novgorod Kremlin. Thirteen rectangular and circular towers ran the length of the walls. Five gate-towers were protected with drawbridges and one of them (Dmitrovskaya) with an *otvodnaya strel'nitsa* as well. The kremlin of Nizhni Novgorod has another distinctive feature – it has flues built in the *pechuras* of the towers and it lacks any machicolation. Other peculiarities of the kremlin include a wall running down a steep slope in ledges and a clock tower with a wooden superstructure.

Novgorod the Great Kremlin

The first fortress was built in Novgorod in 1044 and consisted of a *detinets* (citadel) fortified with a wooden log wall standing on a formidable rampart. Stone walls began to be erected in 1302. The work went on for about 130 years and the construction of a stone *detinets* was only completed in the 1430s. In 1450 it was substantially repaired and in 1484–99 completely rebuilt to meet the challenge of gunpowder artillery. The Novgorod *detinets* was also hugely influenced by the Moscow Kremlin, and an Italian architect may even have taken part in its construction. The walls were 1,385m long, 8.5–10.6m high and 2.7–3.3m thick. Made of stone and faced with brick, they were crowned with a parapet with swallow's-tail merlons. There were probably 13 towers (six

An inside view of the wall surrounding the kremlin of Novgorod the Great. Arches inside walls became very common in the 15th–16th centuries. Some of the arches had chambers (*pechuras*) where cannon were emplaced.

of them gate-towers) placed along the perimeter; however, only nine have been preserved. Some of the towers were rectangular, some circular. Surprisingly, the gate-towers of the Novgorod *detinets* were considerably weaker than those in other kremlin – there were neither *otvodnaya strel'nitsa*, nor 90-degree turns in the passages. The gates tended to be the simplest structures possible, allowing a direct passage into the kremlin. In the course of the 17th century the fortifications of the Novgorod Kremlin (*detinets*) were reconstructed more than once with rectangular merlons replacing the swallow's-tail ones, *podoshvenny boy* loopholes added and several towers modernized.

Tula Kremlin

The fortifications surviving to this day were built as a stronghold to protect the route to Moscow against Tatar raids. Later on a town grew round the fortress and the stronghold developed into a kremlin. The first fortress, built in 1507–09, was made of wood but as early as 1514–20 it was replaced by a masonry one. The basement was laid of white stone and the upper levels of red brick. The walls were 10.3m high and 2.8–3.2m thick and as with most kremlins of the 16th century, which were strongly influenced by Moscow, they were crowned by a parapet with swallow's-tail merlons and had wide arches on the inside. These arches sheltered *podoshvenny boy* loopholes. Nine three- and four-storey towers with machicolations stood along the perimeter. The kremlin was surrounded by a moat with drawbridges at the gates. The ground in front of the kremlin walls was left undeveloped to a distance of 202m to give the defenders a clear field of fire.

Ivangorod Fortress

The fortress of Ivangorod was built in 1492 on the bank of the Narva River, just opposite Rugodiva Fortress (Narva). The fortress had the form of a regular rectangle with four square towers on its corners. It was the first absolutely 'regular' fortress in Russia. The towers, however, did not jut beyond the curtain far enough for them to be used for flanking fire. In consequence, it took the Swedish troops a mere week to seize the fortress in 1496. Having captured the fortress, the Swedes did not stay long in it and withdrew taking 300 prisoners along with them. In the same year the Russians completely rebuilt the fortress in less than three months. The old fortress was restored and another rectangular fortress, eight times as large, added to the eastern side. In the 17th century this became known as Bol'shoi Boyarshi Gorod. Four circular towers were placed on its corners with rectangular ones in between. All the towers projected beyond the curtains and this allowed effective flanking fire to be conducted from them. Some of the towers were equipped with drawbridges that barred the entrance from the wall-walk. The walls were 12–19m high and 3m thick. The fortress was further enlarged in 1507 when a new fortification known as the Zamok (castle) was added on its western side. The Zamok's walls were erected in such a way that the old fortress of 1492 found itself in the centre of the new structure. Two new circular towers were added to the wall close to the Narva River. One of them, the Kolodeznaya Tower, had an unusual design in that a tunnel led from it to a well (*tainik*) that also had two tiers of loopholes commanding the riverbank. Thus, the structure comprised a well and a kind of a caponier. Even today it is possible to go down a stone staircase to the water level and examine the well and the loopholes. Intensive works aimed at bringing the fortifications of Ivangorod to perfection went on during the whole of the 16th century. In 1581 the fortress was seized by the Swedes though in 1590 it was won back by the Russians. The site was further enlarged in 1610 when the Peredni Gorod was enclosed within the fortress's defences by the addition of a wall with two towers. At the same time a fortress rampart adjoining this part of the fortress was erected. It was later faced with masonry. In accordance with the peace treaty of 1617 the fortress passed to Sweden but

Ivangorod Fortress, 1492–1610. Built in 1492, this fortress was small in size and square in shape (1); in 1496 it was rebuilt and considerably enlarged by the addition of a spacious eastern section called Bol'shoi Boyarshi Gorod (2). Another fortification was added in 1507 enclosing the square fortress of 1492. It was called Zamok (the castle, 3). The site was further enlarged in 1610 when the Peredni Gorod (front town, 4) was added to the fortress. At the same time a rampart adjoining this part of the fortress was erected (5); it was later faced with masonry.

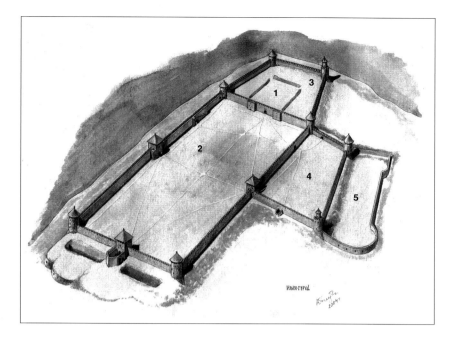

in 1704 it was taken by Russian troops and has belonged to Russia ever since. In 1944 the retreating Nazis blew up six of the towers, but they have now been largely restored. All of the fortifications have preserved their 16–17th-century appearance and the remains of the fortress of 1492 are also visible.

Kopor'e Fortress

The fortress was first mentioned in 1240 when German knights built a wooden castle here. In the following year it was captured and destroyed by a Novgorod army under the command of Alexander Nevsky. The Russians built their own wooden fortress here in 1279. Located on the border between the Russian principalities and the lands of the Teutonic Order, the fortress was of great strategic importance. For that reason, in 1280, the wooden fortress was replaced by a stone one. The people of Novgorod, however, having expelled their prince, destroyed the fortress that symbolized his rule. They were quick to realize their mistake, and in 1297 erected a new stone fortress on the same site.

The bridge over the moat and the gate of Kopor'e Fortress. The gate is built in the wall between two side towers, which is very unusual for Russia as gates in Russian fortresses were usually in gate-towers.

From the second half of the 14th century the strategic significance of the fortress weakened, particularly following the erection of the fortress of Yam-Gorod. In the 16th century, however, with Moscow striving for an outlet to the Baltic Sea, the fortress once more occupied a position of great strategic importance. In 1520–25 it was rebuilt to meet the challenge of gunpowder artillery. Its surviving fortifications date mainly from that time, though fragments of an older wall (1297) can still be seen on some sites along the edge of the hill. The fortress has four towers, with two of them flanking the gateway. Typical of European fortifications, this structure is absolutely unique in Russia where fortress gates were always to be found in gate-towers. The other two towers of the fortress of Kopor'e were located at the most dangerous sections of the wall and perfectly suited for the installation of artillery. Another wall curves along the edge of the hill. There is not a single tower here capable of bringing flanking fire upon the enemy. The fortifications of this part appear rather weak for the period, though the builders may have considered the steep slope of the hill to be a sufficient natural protection. The fortress had two *tainiks* providing the garrison with water: an old one dating from the 13th century, and one built in the 16th century. The complicated system of passages in the two towers flanking the gatehouse is very peculiar indeed. The towers and some parts of the walls have now been restored.

Ladoga Fortress

Ladoga is one of the ten most ancient Russian towns recorded in the annals and the fortress sprang up there some time in the 8th or 9th century AD. The first fortress built here was made of wood, but as early as 1114 (and possibly as far back as the 9th century AD) a stone fortress was erected. It was one of the first – if not the first – stone fortresses in the north of Russia. In the 1490s the fortress was substantially rebuilt to counter artillery fire. Five 16–19m-high three-storeyed artillery towers served as defensive strongpoints. The walls were 7.2–12.0m high and extremely thick (up to 7m) although the fortress was not large, with a perimeter of only 257m. Fortifications of this date, as well as some remains of the ancient walls of the 12th century, still remain to this day; three out of the five towers lie in ruins. In 1585–86 timber-and-earth fortifications were built on to the southern part of the fortress. They consisted of a rampart with three bastions. A *tarassy* wall broken by three towers stretched along the top of the rampart. It is one of the earliest examples of Russian fortifications with bastions. Nothing survives from these fortifications except for a few fragments of the ramparts.

A general view of Ladoga Fortress. It had five towers, some of them round, some rectangular.

Oreshek Fortress

The remains of the Oreshek that survive to this day date from 1514–25 when the previous fortress was fully dismantled and a new one erected in its place. The new fortress had seven towers – six circular and one rectangular – and a citadel of three towers, which was erected and surrounded with a moat that also served as a harbour. The fortress walls were 12m high and 4.5m thick; the citadel walls were as high as 13–14m; the towers were 14–16m high. In 1612 the fortress was seized by the Swedes and renamed Noteburg. In 1702 a Russian Army led by Peter I captured the fortress by assault and renamed it Shlisselburg. Immediately after that, it was fortified with earthwork bastions built in front of each tower; these were faced with masonry in the mid-18th century.

Pskovo-Pechorski Nunnery

The nunnery was founded in 1472 and by the 16th century it had grown wealthy enough to engage in extensive building projects. In 1553–65 it was surrounded by stone walls bolstered by nine towers. Its walls were 726m long and about 2m thick. A hundred *strel'tsy*, together with their families, were brought to live here in order to defend the nunnery. The nunnery is situated on the slopes of a ravine, which has a brook running along the bottom of it, and the fortifications have been integrated into the landscape so that the walls are terraced down the slope. The Pskovo-Pechorski Nunnery protected the western approaches to Pskov. Because of its strategic importance it underwent a number of sieges during the 16th and 17th centuries of which a two-month siege in 1581 by a detachment of Stephen Batory's army was the hardest to endure. The nunnery, however, withstood that siege, as well as many others. In 1701, with the beginning of the Northern War, the nunnery was fortified with ramparts and bastions constructed in front of the masonry walls and towers by order of Peter the Great, and it managed to withstand four successive Swedish assaults.

Troitse-Sergiev Monastery

The monastery was founded in 1345, burned down by the Tatars in 1408 and restored in 1411. In 1540–50 it was encircled by 1,370m-long masonry walls, along with 11 towers. These walls were only 5.5–6.0m high, but almost 3.5m thick. Thanks to its formidable fortifications the monastery withstood a 16-month siege laid by the Polish-Lithuanian armies in 1608–10. In the mid-17th century its defensive fortifications were completely rebuilt: the walls became

Fortifications of the Pskovo-Pechorski Nunnery. The nunnery stands on two hills divided by a small river, as a result, the walls have to go down to the river and then up the other side of the hill.

View of the city wall of Pskov from the town. The fortifications were built early in the 16th century and withstood several tenacious sieges. Today, some sections of the wall have been restored and give a fair notion of what the city fortifications looked like in the 16th and 17th centuries.

twice as high and thick as they were before, the number of levels of loophole was increased from two to three, and the height of the towers was also raised. Four octagonal towers were placed on the corners with seven rectangular ones in between. It is mainly the fortifications of this period that can be seen to this day.

Urban fortifications of Pskov

The citadel (*krom*) of Pskov dates from the medieval period but the defensive walls that protected the trading quarter (*possad*) belong to the end of the 15th and the first half of the 16th centuries, when the wooden wall was replaced with a masonry one. By the 1670s Pskov was encircled by several lines of formidable masonry walls. The external walls were 6.5m high and 4–6m thick. Thirty-seven towers were erected along the perimeter, equipped with *sluhs* in order to detect enemy engineering works.

Urban fortifications of Smolensk

The town of Smolensk has been in existence since the 9th century AD. In the 11th and 12th centuries wooden walls placed on earth ramparts surrounded it. In the 15th century the Lithuanians seized Smolensk and rebuilt its defensive fortifications. In 1514 the town was annexed by the state of Moscow. As it was of great strategic importance for Moscow, Smolensk had its defensive fortifications repeatedly rebuilt in the course of the 16th century. The surviving fortifications date mainly from the end of the 16th century. An armistice with Poland was to come to an end in 1603, and with war imminent the decision was taken to carry out an urgent modernization of the fortifications of Smolensk, which was done in 1595–1602. The general extent of the walls reached 6,575m, which enclosed most of the town. These fortifications cannot be described as either a kremlin or a military fortress. They are just town fortifications, comparable, however, in their power with a fortress. The walls were 8.5–12.8m high and 3–7.5m thick. As in the Moscow Kremlin, the walls and towers were crowned with a parapet with swallow's-tail merlons. For the first time in Russia, both *podoshvenny boy* and *sredni boy* loopholes pierced the walls. Thirty-eight towers, including nine gate-towers, were distributed along the perimeter. It is worth noting that no gates were built in the western wall of the fortress, the one facing towards the Polish-Lithuanian border. Most of them were concentrated on the northern side, facing the suburbs. The average length of the curtain wall between towers was 158m and the towers themselves were of two types – rectangular and polygonal. As they were the strongpoints of the defence, they were provided with machicolations as well as ordinary loopholes. A number of towers and gate-towers were further protected by timber-and-earth fortifications on the exterior along with underground galleries (*sluhs*) for the detection of enemy mining works.

Linear defensive systems

The Bereg line

The first attempts to protect the southern borders of Russia from the Tatars date back to the 14th century when the first *zasekas* were positioned on potential invasion routes. A *zaseka* was a heap of cut-down trees cut in such a way that their tops and branches jutted out in the direction of the enemy.

In the 15th century a defence system known as the Bereg was built on the line of the river Oka. There is no evidence that the Bereg was a continuous system of fortifications. It is more likely that it was conceived as a line of powerful fortresses (Kolomna, Alexin, Peremyshl', Tarusa, Kashira, Serpukhov, Kaluga), populated by strong garrisons. River crossing sites between these fortresses were blocked by stakes driven into the riverbed. The Bereg line was ungarrisoned until 1472 when an 180,000-strong force was moved into the area. However, this was not a permanent garrison at this point and troops were only moved in when there was a threat of invasion. It wasn't until 1569 that several regiments were billeted here on a permanent basis. In 1599 the garrisons along the Bereg line were moved southwards and positioned along the Zasechnaya Cherta.

The Zasechnaya Cherta

The Zasechnaya Cherta was developed from a loose association of fortified villages, towns, field fortifications and *zasekas* that grew up throughout the 15th and 16th centuries in response to Tatar incursions. By the second half of the 16th century this loose network had become an unbroken line of defences. The Zasechnaya Cherta now consisted of a series of well-fortified towns, natural

The gate-tower of the Nikolo-Korel'ski Monastery. The monastery was founded in the 15th century at the place where the river Severnaya Dvina discharges into the White Sea. The tower was built in 1692 on the site of a monastery gate that had burned down in 1690. In 1932 the tower was transferred to Kolomenskoye Park in Moscow where one can see it today.

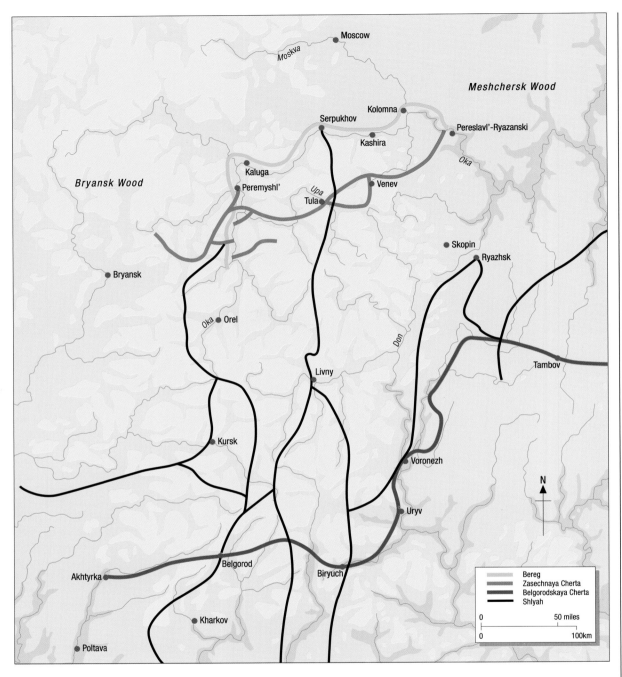

barriers (rivers, brooks, ravines), *zasekas*, ditches, ramparts with palisades and specially built wooden fortresses with garrisons billeted in them. The fortresses along the Zasechnaya Cherta made active use of local geography – confluences of river, marshland, ravines, hills, etc. They were often built on a hillock on a cape at the confluence of two rivers or brooks. Thus the fortress resembled a triangle, two sides of which were protected by natural barriers (rivers, brooks or ravines), and only the landward side had to be additionally fortified. This most vulnerable side was provided with a multi-tiered defence consisting of three lines of ramparts with a palisade. The first, the lowest external rampart was manned with riflemen, the second and the third (overhanging the second)

The defence lines of south Russia in the 16th and 17th centuries: the Bereg (yellow), the Zasechnaya Cherta (red) the Belgorodskaya Cherta (blue) and the main routes (*shlyah*) along which the Tatars made their raids on Russia (black).

The view from the Kokui Tower of the kremlin of Novgorod the Great. One can easily see shingle-covered walls and towers.

with riflemen and artillery. The ramparts were bow shaped allowing the men to provide 'fan-like' covering fire, which was particularly crucial given the inaccurate nature of gunpowder weaponry at the time. The other sides of the fortress were protected by natural barriers; their defences were less sophisticated and often consisted of only a rampart with a palisade. The gates in these fortresses were mostly built in the centre of the landward side or at one of the corners. Although this location was easiest to attack, it was also the most logical position for making sorties against the mobile Tatar cavalry.

As long as the frontier guard service functioned adequately, Tatar breakthroughs were uncommon, though they raided every year. However, in the early 17th century Russia found itself enveloped in the *smoota* (time of troubles) followed by a Polish and Swedish invasion. The frontier guard service along the Zasechnaya Cherta fell into decay as the troops were transferred to face the threats from other directions and the Tatars were quick to take advantage of the situation. Between 1607 and 1616 their hordes, sometimes 100,000 strong, made yearly (with the exception of 1612) raids penetrating through the Zasechnaya Cherta, ravaging towns and entire regions, sometimes even reaching the environs of Moscow. Moreover, not content with making brief raids, the Tatars did not retire to their steppes in winter but plundered the Russian lands all year round now.

The frontier guard service was reestablished in the year 1613, though war with Poland and Sweden did not allow Moscow to detach considerable forces for the protection of the southern border. For example, in 1616 there were only 3,000 soldiers based there, which was not enough to defend such an extensive section of the border. Just as the situation began to improve in the 1620s war with Poland for the possession of Smolensk (1632–34) broke out. Again some of the border forces had to be withdrawn from the south and the Tatars again jumped at the opportunity to break through the Zasechnaya Cherta sowing death and destruction. On top of other calamities the Tatar raids led to the desertion from under the walls of Smolensk of southern soldiers, who sought to defend their families from the Tatars rather than fight the Poles.

In 1635 the task of fortifying the southern borders was reorganized and a new defensive line was built. This was of a larger extent than the Zasechnaya

Cherta; it was further to the south and known as the Belgorodskaya Cherta. The older defensive lines were also renovated and by 1638 Russia had three fully functioning defensive lines – the Bereg, the Zasechnaya Cherta and the Belgorodskaya Cherta. At the same time the frontier guard service was reorganized and many new frontier towns were built and populated. Finally, the Russian Army went over to the offensive against the Crimean Tatars. From 1648 onwards there was no large-scale Tatar incursion into southern Russia.

Construction

All the defensive lines described above had a similar structure. They consisted of a line of natural barriers (rivers, brooks, ravines), timber obstructions (*zaseka*), a series of ramparts and ditches on open ground as well as logs dug into the ground and leaning in the direction of the enemy (*nadolby*) and palisades (*chastokol*). These lines were also based on a series of fixed fortifications that were provided with garrisons.

Taking the Zasechnaya Cherta as an example; it ran roughly parallel to the Oka River and extended over 1,000km from the Bryansk to the Mestchersk forests, which themselves provided a formidable obstacle to cavalry. The Tatars followed traditional invasion routes known as *shlyah*, and they could not pass through these dense forests. The section of the line between Tula and Venev was believed to be the most dangerous one as the Muravsky *shlyah*, which led straight to Moscow, passed through this area and was a favourite invasion route for the Tatars, so the line in this place was of a double thickness.

As the area was so heavily forested it is hardly surprising that a large part of the Zasechnaya Cherta consisted of timber obstructions (*zaseka*) – the very name 'Zasechnaya Cherta' derives from the word *zaseka*. There were a number of procedures to creating one of these wooden obstacles. Firstly, trees were felled a few metres from the edge of the forest so that the *zaseka* was concealed by what looked to be regular growth. Secondly, the trees were cut about 2m up so that the trunks fell in the direction that that zaseka was designed to block, with the fallen trunks lying over the stumps. Although a *zaseka* was an insurmountable barrier for cavalry, it had one main drawback – it was extremely vulnerable to fire. Local villagers were strictly forbidden to take fire (torches, candles, etc.) near a *zaseka*, let alone build a fire; occasionally they were forbidden to go into the forest at all. The Tatars would deliberately use fire to destroy old *zasekas*, or sometimes whole sections of the forest, though waiting for the fire to die back enough so that the area could be crossed could take a long time. Special patrols regularly checked on the condition of *zasekas* and the slightest irregularities (e.g. a fresh path) would be put right by building new obstructions.

The fortresses, those strongpoints on which the Zasechnaya Cherta was based, could be divided into three types. The first type included the old fortresses that dated from the 16th century. These fortifications tended to be somewhat old-fashioned and often had problems with their water supplies.

The second type comprised fortresses built across roads in order to bar traffic. They were rectangular in plan and had a gate-tower on the side looking towards the direction of the enemy. In the 16th century, gate-towers, closed on each side, equipped for self-defence, and provided with a watch-turret on top, were the only defensive fortifications on the roads. In the 17th century, forts (*ostrog*) emerged around gate-towers; they were usually enclosed by plain walls in the shape of vertical palisades (*stoyachi ostrog*). On the inner side the palisade had wooden planking (*krovat'*) with handrails and a short flight of stairs, which was used as a wall-walk where riflemen were placed during battle. Artillery was positioned on specially piled-up earth platforms. Occasionally, in fortresses that were particularly often subject to the Tatar attack, the walls were made of logs (*tarassy*-type) with or without a filling of earth. The side of a fortress liable to be directly attacked during a siege got additional defences: a ditch was dug

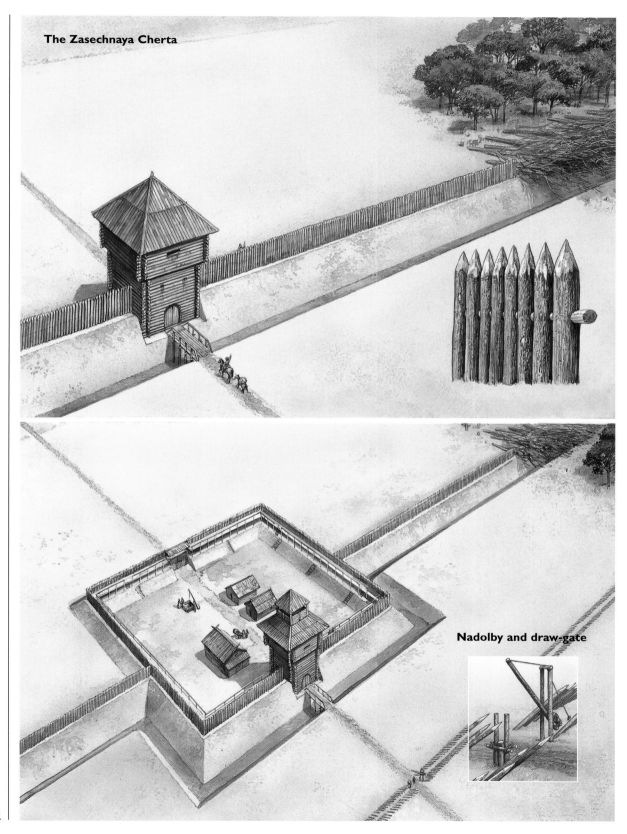

The Zasechnaya Cherta

Nadolby and draw-gate

The Zazechnaya Cherta

A linear defensive work of the 16th (above) and 17th (below) centuries. The importance of securing the southern borders of Russia from Tatar raids had long been realized and temporary *zasekas* (heaps of slashed trees) were placed on enemy pathways from the 12th centur onwards. The 15th century saw a new defence system called the Bereg built. This was not a continuous line of defence works: stress was laid on obstructing the main roads and building strong fortresses with a permanent garrison. The 16th century was marked by the appearance of a continuous line of fortifications – the Zasechnaya Cherta. The defences consisted of *zasekas* and palisades and the roads were blocked with gate-towers. In the 17th century the fortifications of the Zasechnaya Cherta were replaced by fortresses whose walls were either palisades or, at more perilous locations, *tarassy*-style structures. The approaches to the fortresses were protected by ditches and *nadolby* (logs dug into the ground and leaning in the direction of the enemy). In the 17th century the fortifications of the Zasechnaya Cherta were modernized: gate-towers were replced by fortresses and fortress walls.

and a palisade was stood on a rampart. The road led across a drawbridge or a narrow bridge, which could be easily destroyed, then through the gate-tower, with generally a double gate and sometimes a portcullis, and came out on the internal, safer side through a gate that was much more primitive, without a gate-tower. These fortresses were relatively small with a few (three or four) peasant houses (*izba*), a powder depot and a well. The garrison generally consisted of 150–200 men, though they only stayed in the fortress in spring and summer when the Tatars made their raids. In autumn and winter they were billeted in neighbouring villages. This type of fortress generally had better water supplies as they were not built on the top of hills. Various methods of water supply were provided for these fortifications: wells, brooks, tanks and secret passages leading to rivers (*tainik*). The fortresses were flanked by ditches and earth ramparts with palisades, which extended as far as the *zasekas*. The place around the fortress was cleared of everything within a radius of at least 100m to deprive the enemy of cover and prevent their setting fire to the fortress. Fire was a constant threat, so not only were the forests and bushes cleared near a fortress, but even the grass was carefully cut back.

The third type of fortress was an earth or timber-and-earth fortification consisting of ditches and ramparts with bastions (pentagonal fortifications), ravelins (triangular fortifications) and redoubts (close field fortifications usually square in shape). These fortresses were deliberately built as weapon emplacements for artillery. They were built on open ground, unprotected by natural defences, in particularly dangerous places. The construction of bastions, ravelins and redoubts was not needed to protect the fortress from artillery fire, as the Tatars had none. It was rather the desire of the Russians to use their own artillery efficiently – the straight earth ramparts of the previous

The gallery behind the parapet (wall-walk) in the Kazan Kremlin. Historically, the *boevoy hod* (wall-walk) in all fortresses had wooden roofs. The roofs haven't survived and now can only be seen where they have been reconstructed, as here.

43

style of fortresses did not allow for accurate flanking fire. Fortresses were connected by a system of ditches and ramparts. Comparatively small flat embankments for artillery (*raskat*) were built on the inside along the ramparts, at a distance of 30–100m from one another. They were 4–4.5m wide and inclined 12–15 degrees inside. *Raskats* were reached by an inclined embankment, the entrance being always on the southern side. The soldiers on the ramparts were protected by gabions (*turs*) filled with earth and a hurdle. The ramparts between fortresses also incorporated bastions as well as ravelins and redoubts placed in front of the ramparts. The entire system of fortifications here was based on strict cooperation between separate weapon emplacements.

The approaches to all these types of fortress were provided with additional barriers such as wolf-holes, ditches, earthen ramparts, dams, river crossings blocked with stakes driven into the riverbed or logs with thorns, *nadolby*, and lowered gates. *Nadolby*, sharpened stakes fixed into the ground facing the likely direction of an enemy approach, were usually positioned in two rows. Draw-gates were logs fixed on two pillars placed along road edges. At the approach of an enemy the log was lowered and barred the road. The structure resembled a modern barrier. Draw-gates put in line with *nadolby* were designed to stem the advance of the Tatar cavalry on the approaches to a fortress, thus allowing its defenders time to prepare for defence (draw up or destroy the bridge, arrange the riflemen on the walls, etc). Sometimes watch-towers were put on the approaches to a fortress so that the garrison would know of the enemy's advance in good time.

In the 17th century the Zasechnaya Cherta consisted of two lines of defence. The fortresses with all the barriers described above (*zaseka*, ramparts, ditches, *nadolby*, palisades, etc.) constituted only the internal defence line. At a distance of about 40–60km from it was the external line of fortifications, consisting of the same kind of barriers with the exception of fortresses. The external line of defences was designed to slow the Tatar approach, if not stop it altogether, and give the defenders time to prepare the internal line to counter the threat.

A linear defensive system of this extent required a well-designed system of communication for it to be truly effective. Light signals were sent from one fortress to another from the neighbouring hills. Special watch detachments of several men were on duty in the woods – two or three men sitting up in a tree, two or three mounted orderlies keeping watch under the tree, ready to gallop to the fortress any moment. Upon sight of the enemy the watchmen in the tree set fire to a piece of birch-bark soaked in tar sending a smoke signal, while the mounted orderlies galloped to the fortress at top speed to give more detailed information about enemy strength.

Another method of fighting the Tatars was to set fire to the steppe so that the grass was burnt over vast areas. This deprived the Tatars' horses of pasture and was one of the earliest ways the Russians found of combating them, dating from the 16th century.

From the 1640s onwards the Tatars only raided the Belgorodskaya Cherta in places where its construction had not yet been completed. After the entire construction was completed in 1646, Tatar raids on Russian land stopped. Nonetheless, the internal defensive lines were not neglected and repair work was carried out on the Zasechnaya Cherta through to the late 17th century (1659, 1666, 1676–79). The importance of protecting the southern frontier was still recognized in the 18th century, as can be shown by the construction of the Orenburg and Dnieper lines.

The object of all these linear defensive systems was to impede the advance of the Tatars, restrict the manoeuvrability of their cavalry, and gain time to allow the civilian population to be evacuated and large forces to be summoned from nearby fortresses. The Tatars had no siege machinery or great knowledge of siege warfare, so unsophisticated earth and earth-and-timber fortifications served the purpose well, and were cheap to build.

The living sites

The kremlin accommodated the prince's or *voivode*'s court, the *prikaznaya izba* (office), barns, a powder-magazine, a prison and other public buildings. A cathedral was an indispensable element of every kremlin. In large centres the kremlin could even incorporate a monastery and a great deal of importance was attached to food storehouses. The largest section of a kremlin was taken up by the *osadnye dvory* (sing. *osadny dvor*) and *osadnye kleti* (sing. *osadnaya klet'*) – small residential buildings that were also used for protecting valuable property during a siege. The population of most towns, including the elite, lived outside the kremlin walls but noblemen and *deti boyarskie* (lesser gentry in military service), as well as monasteries, had *osadnye dvory*; these tended to be small (*c*.100m^2) when compared with the more palatial residences in the *possad* but big enough to serve as living quarters. The rest of the population had to make do with *osadnye kleti*, which were much smaller than the *osadnye dvory* – the ones in Tula are known to have been about 3 × 3m. They were low huts built of logs clustered close to each other and usually found near the central square and the church, so that during a siege the civilian population would not get in the way of the military defending the kremlin walls. The only people who lived permanently in a kremlin were those in service in the prince's court or bishop's house, the clergy and the garrison.

Next to the kremlin, often just outside the main gate, was the *torg* (market place), with the main entrance to the kremlin looking on it. The wall of the kremlin facing the market place was always the most decorated of the various walls; thus the Spasskaya Tower in Moscow's Kremlin facing the market place (the site of today's Red Square) is the most colourful of the towers of the Kremlin.

The centre of the kremlin usually held the prince's or *voivode*'s court, the cathedral, and the bishop's court. This arrangement can be seen in quite a number of 16th-century kremlins. The main street of the kremlin connected this complex with the gate leading to the market place. On either side of this street was a market place for use during sieges, an office, a powder magazine, a prison, and other public buildings. As often as not the main street was the only street within the kremlin walls, but there could sometimes be other smaller streets or one or two perpendicular streets. In this case the central complex was at the junction of these streets.

Churches and monasteries had no fixed places in the kremlin. They often stood in the corners or near a gate, where they 'blessed' the entrance. A small military fort (*ostrog*) would often only have a chapel in the gatehouse. The chapel was positioned over the entrance and played the same role as churches by kremlin gates. Where there were no churches near the gate-tower an icon was often hung over the gate.

In order to provide a fortress with water wells or secret underground passages to rivers (*tainik*) were dug. The outlet of these passages was located a short distance from the river itself, where a well could be easily dug. From the late 15th century this secret passage was often built into the tower nearest to the river, called the *tainichnaya* tower. Sometimes a fortress was deliberately built on a brook or spring so that the garrison would never go thirsty. However, it was not safe to rely on one source of water supply – a *tainik* could be discovered by the enemy or a brook drained. So, as a rule, fortresses would have at least two different water sources and, as a last resort, water was stored in tanks. Wells, the entrances to *tainik* and tanks of water were carefully guarded; a well in Mozhaisk is known to have been enclosed by a strong fence.

Provisions were kept in barns or towers. For example, one of the towers of Ivangorod was called the Proviantskaya (provisions) Tower. In some fortresses there were Porokhovye (powder) towers, which held stores of gunpowder in their basements; powder magazines were more common though.

Fire was a great threat to fortresses during this period; wooden fortresses were particularly vulnerable though stone fortresses could also be badly damaged as wood was widely used in the construction of these fortifications. Various preventive measures were taken to protect against fire: work involving fire was only done on the outskirts of a town; burning wood in stoves was forbidden during summer, and tubs of water were kept near stoves at all other times. Every resident also had 'fire duty' to do – one man out of every dozen was to be on duty each night. There were also permanent fire brigades equipped with barrels, fire engines, buckets, axes, hooks and other tools. Even *strel'tsy* were enlisted to fight fire. Special watchmen were on round-the-clock duty in kremlins, and would inform the population of a fire by ringing the bells.

In contrast to kremlins, the majority of the population of border fortresses lived permanently within the fortress walls. Many of these fortresses were populated by *strel'tsy* (sing. *strelets*), regular Russian soldiers of the 16th and 17th centuries.

The numerical strength of a garrison depended on the strategic significance of a fortress. In large cities the garrison could consist of hundreds of men, while in small fortresses during peacetime a garrison could be as small as a dozen men. As a rule, a garrison consisted of *strel'tsy*, noblemen and *deti boyarskie*, gunners, gate-guards and, less commonly, Cossacks. Detachments of foreign mercenaries could be enlisted as well.

In the case of a potential siege martial law was introduced in the fortress, the fortress gates were locked, with the keys being handed over to the *voivode*. Powder magazines were taken special care of and the sale of alcohol was prohibited, with all the *kabaks* (sing. *kabak*, bar) closed except those owned by the state. Refugees were kept under close observation; foreigners and peasants from frontier villages were not allowed into the fortress for fear of treason, though women and young children were always given refuge.

The Kazan Kremlin. It is the only Russian kremlin with a mosque, though it was only built in the 20th century.

Garrison personnel of some fortresses

Town	Year	Strel'tsy	Gunners	Others	Total numerical strength of a garrison
Gdov	1585–88	100	11	5 gate-guards	116
Izborsk	1585–88	100	15	2 gate-guards	117
Ostrov	1585–88	100	20	2 gate-guards	122
Opochka	1585–88	100	34	6 gate-guards	140
Sebezh	1585–88	54	31	15 gate-guards and 137 Cossacks	237
Smolensk	1607	1,700	200	1,600 noblemen and *deti boyarskie*	3,500
Novgorod the Great	1626	564	20	1,297 noblemen, *deti boyarskie* and others – Cossacks and armed peasants	2,752
Ladoga	1626				289
Porkhov	1626				75
Pskov	1626				4,807

The Proviantskaya (provisions) Tower and the wall-walk of the fortress of Ivangorod. The tower was used for storing foodstuffs, hence its name.

The sites at war

The main siege techniques of the period in question consisted of digging mine galleries to undermine walls and setting up artillery batteries to breach walls with gunfire. Siege machinery had lost its importance in Russia by the mid-15th century as by that point wooden siege engines, like rams, siege towers, etc., were easily destroyed by defensive artillery fire. To withstand aggressive artillery fire, fortress walls and towers became lower and thicker and gunpowder artillery was along the length of the walls. Surprise sorties, aimed at destroying enemy batteries and mine galleries, were an important part of siege warfare, as were *sluhs*, underground tunnels used to detect mine galleries, which were driven out from the fortress walls.

The way that fortresses of the period withstood sieges can be best illustrated by the examples of the defence of Pskov in 1581 and 1615 and Smolensk in 1609–11.

Pskov 1581

By the end of the 16th century Pskov was one the most powerful fortresses not only in Russia, but in all of Eastern Europe. Beyond the citadel (*krom*), it was defended by several lines of formidable town fortifications. Its garrison consisted of 12,000–15,000 men (2,500 *strel'tsy*, 500 Cossacks, the rest militia).

View through one of the loopholes of Kopor'e Fortress. Note how convenient it is for flanking fire.

On 18 August 1581, a 47,000-strong Polish Army led by Stephen Batory approached the town and placed it under siege. The defenders first act was to build earth fortifications (trenches, dugouts, gabions) and mount 20 cannon. On 7 September the Poles brought continuous artillery fire to bear upon the town fortifications from their batteries which went on until the following morning. As a result a curtain of about 150m long was breached in several places and the Pokrovskaya Tower was completely destroyed. The defence, however, had managed to erect wooden log walls filled with earth (built in the *tarassy* style) behind the breached masonry walls. At 5.00am on 8 September Stephen Batory's army attempted to assault the breach and the defenders sounded the alarm bell and opened fire from all their cannon. The numerically superior Poles managed to cross the ditch, reach the breach and capture two broken towers, though they failed to break through the newly built wooden walls. According to an annalist, the defenders fought bravely. 'some stood by the wall with spears, *strel'tsy* shot their arquebuses, *deti boyarskie* shot arrows from their bows, others threw stones'. Then, Voivode Shuisky, commander of the garrison, launched a counter-attack. Holy icons were brought out to the breach and the town's heavenly protectors were appealed to, then the fighting began. Kegs with powder were rolled into the captured towers and blown up there together with the enemy

The passageway down to the well in the Kolodeznaya (well) Tower of Ivangorod Fortress. There were two similar stairways on either side of the tower. This allowed quite a number of people to fetch water simultaneously and ensured that the defenders had access to the well if one of the staircases was damaged.

settled inside. A sortie was launched, by both men and women; the Poles were routed and put to flight. The Poles had lost about 5,000 men; the Russians 863 killed and 1,626 wounded. Once they had reoccupied the positions the defenders fortified the wooden walls, dug a ditch between the wooden wall and the remains of the masonry one and drove stakes into the ground all along the perimeter of the breach. The Poles continued to assault the walls – sometimes as many as two or three times a day, as well as by night.

Batory called on the besieged to surrender but the answer was a firm refusal, so the besiegers changed their tactics and turned to subterranean warfare. They started digging nine tunnels at the same time; the besieged responded by building counter-tunnels and an underground war was launched. On 23 September, the defenders blew up two of the Polish mine galleries while the rest caved in by themselves. The Poles decided to change their tactics again and, on 24 October, they began to fire red-hot shot into the town hoping to set it on fire. However, special town fire brigades quickly poured water on the balls and put out any fires as soon as they started. Then the Poles undertook rather a desperate attempt to sap the wall at its base. On 28 October under the cover of artillery fire a large detachment, protecting themselves with large siege shields, rushed to the wall and began to destroy the lower part of the masonry with pickaxes and crowbars. The defenders opened fire with handguns and poured tar, pitch and boiling water down onto the Poles, only a few of whom escaped alive.

During the following five days Stephen Batory's army constantly bombarded the walls of Pskov. They managed to breach the wall facing the Velikaya River and on 2 November assaulting columns of the Polish Army rushed to attack the breaches across the frozen river. The attackers were met, however, with such effective and powerful artillery fire that they were halted and then routed. Finally, on 6 November, Batory gave up his attempts to take the town by assault and decided to starve the defenders to death. The situation in Pskov rapidly became desperate, and attempts from outside to resupply the town were frustrated by the blockade; only one string of carts loaded with provisions and convoyed by 300 *strel'tsy* managed to steal in through the Polish siege lines. On 1 December Batory left his army and went to Vilno, instructing Hetman Zamoisky to complete the siege. On 4 January, taking advantage of Batory's absence, Voivode Shuisky made a sortie that decided the outcome of the siege; the Poles pulled back from their lines and retired. Throughout the course of the siege the Poles made 31 assaults and the Russian defenders 46 sorties.

Pskov 1615

On 29 July 1615, a Swedish army under the command of the talented general King Gustavus Adolphus approached Pskov and set up their camps in the nearby monasteries. The Swedish Army was 9,080 strong, and contained many English, Scottish, German and French mercenaries. The fortress garrison was 4,220 strong, plus a small detachment of 344 *strel'tsy* who had been sent from Moscow to bolster the defences; the townsfolk and the peasants from the neighbouring villages were also put under arms. In the second half of August, Pskov was entirely blockaded and on 3 September, the long-awaited Swedish siege artillery arrived and was arranged in three batteries located on three sides of the town. The defenders made a continuous series of sorties and managed to kill the Swedish commander Horn and wound the king himself; in the course of another sortie the defenders managed to capture a battery of cannon and kill 300 German mercenaries. On 17 September a massive artillery bombardment of the fortress began and the Swedes successfully managed to destroy the Varlaamskaya and Vysokaya Towers as well as parts of the adjoining walls. In the assault that followed, the Swedes seized the Varlaamskaya Tower but were immediately counter-attacked and dislodged. As disease spread throughout the Swedish Army, Gustavus Adolphus followed the example of Stephen Batory and bombarded the town with red-hot shot, which was as ineffective as it had been in 1581. On 9 October the Swedish king himself led a second attack on the breach in the ill-fated Varlaamskaya Tower. The assault lasted a whole day with the defenders shooting handguns, throwing down logs and stones, and pouring tar and boiling water down on the attackers. The Swedes broke through as far as the gate leading into the town from the Pskova River, and even penetrated into the town itself however, by the end of the day the Swedes had been forced back from the town and the Varlaamskaya Tower. The third assault was planned for 11 October and an intensive artillery barrage was

The Varlaamskaya Tower of the city wall of Pskov. During the siege of Pskov by the Swedish Army in 1615 this tower changed hands more than once.

launched early in the morning. However, one of the cannon blew up taking with it the main powder supply for the army; Gustavus Adolphus cancelled the assault, shipped out his artillery and lifted the siege.

Smolensk 1609–11

In 1609 Sigismund III of Poland laid claim to the Russian throne and invaded Russia. His advance was barred by Smolensk, which defended the western border of the state. The vanguard of the Polish Army arrived outside the walls of the city on 19 September 1609. Realizing that they would not be able to defend the trading quarter (*possad*), the inhabitants burned it down so that it did not provide shelter and building material for the Poles. On the night of 24/25 September, the Poles attempted to storm the fortress and charges were placed against the Kopytenskie and Avraamievskie gates. While the Kopytenskie Gate was hardly damaged by the explosion, the Avraamievskie one was practically destroyed and the way into the fortress was open. Polish troops poured into the breach but the defenders managed to hold them back in a series of desperate hand-to-hand encounters. This unsuccessful assault forced the attackers to resort to a systematic bombardment of the fortress. When a fire broke out in the fortress, the defenders expected a general assault to follow but a truce envoy arrived instead, proposing they should surrender. The Russian defenders refused to give in and the Poles turned to subterranean warfare, digging mines beneath the walls of the fortress. The defenders responded by digging countermines and destroying the enemy's galleries; three Polish tunnels were blown up in January, two in February, and two more in July. The defenders also made continual sorties during this period in an effort to unsettle the attackers. At the end of May the Poles received eight large-calibre cannon from Riga and brought intensive fire to bear upon the Granovitaya Tower, which was soon breached. The Russians just had time to erect an inner log wall of cells filled

Interior view of a chamber (*pechura*) in the bottom tier of the wall (*podoshvenny boy*) of the fortress of Ladoga.

Fighting platform on the top of one of Kopor'e's towers. These platforms could be used for firing handguns or small cannon.

with earth (built in the *tarassy* style) before the attacking Poles, Germans and Hungarians were upon them. They were thrown back by the weight of fire coming from these improvised defences.

Over the next few days this pattern repeated itself: the Polish artillery breached the walls only for the assaulting troops to find the breaches blocked by hastily assembled defences and the attackers were forced back. On 1 December 1610, a mine was detonated destroying a section of wall, only for the Poles to realize that a new section of wall had been constructed behind it, thus rendering their efforts useless. After this setback they once more sought to secure the town through negotiations, but were once again rebuffed and so they began to prepare for a decisive assault. They had learned from deserters about a weak section in the fortress wall. Built in a hurry late in the autumn, that section of the wall was far from solid and it became the main target of both the Polish engineers and artillery. By this point in the siege, spring 1611, the situation in the fortress had become critical. Many of the defenders had died either in fighting or from a severe epidemic of scurvy. The garrison numbered no more than 300–400 men capable of fighting. At dawn on 3 June 1611, four storming columns quietly approached the fortress from different sides. Each column was supplied with special storm ladders so broad that five or six men could climb each ladder simultaneously. Hetman Stephen Pototski himself carried a ladder to set an example to his soldiers, and he was also the first to climb the wall. Although the defenders managed to beat off one attack, they were too small in numbers to repulse so many assaults in different places at the same time. Voivode M. B. Shein was trying to transfer a party of his men to another breach when an explosion sounded by the Kryloshevskie Gate. On the eve of the assault the Poles had been informed by a deserter of the existence of a wide drainpipe (about 8m in diameter) in the adjoining wall and a Maltese knight had laid a mine there. The explosion destroyed a considerable part of the wall, 20–40m, and through that breach the Poles broke through into the town; only Voivode M. B. Shein with his family and 15 soldiers, who had locked themselves in one of the towers, offered a period of resistance. A 20-month siege had turned Smolensk and the surrounding area into a desert and the majority of the local people who had sheltered in the fortress were dead. However, the prolonged siege had also devastated the Polish Army and Sigismund was forced to give up the idea of advancing on Moscow; he disbanded his army and returned to Warsaw.

The sieges described above allow some general conclusions to be drawn about defending Russian fortresses during the period in question. Firstly, in the 'age of powder' successful fortress defence was impossible without military activity on the part of the defenders. Therefore, in the course of a siege the defenders had to

The gate-tower and the passage connecting the tower and the wall of Ivangorod. This tower was protected by a drawbridge placed inside the wall. There was a passageway underneath the bridge and the exit can be seen halfway up the wall.

make frequent sorties in order to destroy the attacker's artillery, manpower or mine galleries, and when an attacker captured any part of the fortification, the defenders needed to counter-attack immediately to force the attacker out before the position could be consolidated. Secondly, the Russians widely used auxiliary timber-and-earth fortifications behind the most vulnerable sections of outer fortifications In many cases those auxiliary fortifications saved the defence in what seemed to be desperate situations. Thirdly, numerous underground galleries (*sluhs*) leading out beyond the fortress walls helped to detect enemy mining works and allow for their neutralization with the help of countermines.

As far as Russian assault tactics for sieges are concerned, the siege of Kazan in 1552 is a particularly interesting example of the siege warfare of the period as it is the first case of a Russian force using extensive trench networks and subterranean warfare, probably learned from the Poles at the siege of Starodub in 1535.

Kazan 1552

The siege of Kazan by the Russian troops under the command of Ivan the Terrible in 1552 was the third Russian campaign against the Tatar capital. In the first campaign (1547) the Russians failed to reach Kazan and turned back. In the second campaign (1549) the army reached Kazan and laid siege to it but was not able to take the town. On 22 August 1552, the Russian Army approached Kazan and had it blockaded by the following evening. All the regiments were ordered to entrench; each soldier was to drive in one stake and every ten soldiers were to make a gabion. On the night of 26 August, the besiegers started to surround the town with two siege lines (circumvallation and contravallation). In order to hamper their work, the defenders made a sortie. The fighting lasted the whole night and it was only by the next morning that the enemy was forced back into the fortress. The earthworks were successfully completed by 29 August and the artillery (about 150 cannon) was arranged in batteries. The river was also diverted away from the town in order to deprive the defenders of drinking water, but they had prepared for this and had access to a nearby spring. On 30 August an intensive artillery bombardment of the town started. Under the supervision of Ivan Vyrodkov a 12m-high battery-tower was built that contained ten heavy, large-calibre cannon and 50 lighter cannon. This tower allowed concentrated fire to be brought to bear upon a small section of the wall as well as a secrtion of the town itself. In all probability, the few cannon of the defence had by that time been put out of action, otherwise the tower would have been a perfect target. The next day, 31 August, the Russians began to excavate four mine galleries simultaneously. The work was done under the supervision of a foreign engineer, Nemchin Rozmysl. The explosion of one of these mines destroyed the tunnel by means of which the defenders were supplied with water, and the lack of fresh water immediately led to an outbreak of disease within the town. By 26 September, in spite of almost daily enemy sorties, the Russians managed to bring their trenches as far as the fortress ditch. At dawn on 2 October all the mine galleries were exploded simultaneously, destroying the wall by the main gates, and the artillery began firing to provide cover for the assaulting troops. The Russians broke into the town and, despite a spirited Tatar counter-attack, Kazan fell.

Tula 1607

At the siege of Tula in 1607 the Russian troops resorted to the rare tactic of flooding enemy fortifications. The town was sheltering a rebel army under the command of I. Bolotnikov. The Tsar's army, led by V. Shuisky, blockaded the town and launched a systematic bombardment from the north and south. During the summer, 22 attempts were made to take the fortress by assault but

Siege of Kazan, 1552

Siege of Kazan, 1552

This plate shows the dramatic siege of Kazan by the troops of Ivan the Terrible in 1552. It was the third campaign of the Russian Army against the Tatar capital. In the first campaign (1547) the Russians failed to reach Kazan and turned back. In the second campaign (1549) the army reached Kazan and laid siege to it, but was not able to take the city. It was only in 1552 that, after careful preparation, the Russian Army captured Kazan by storm with the siege lasting from 23 August to 2 October. The main part in the operation was played by artillery (1) and mines (2). During the first 30 days the Russian troops continuously bombarded the city and a crucial part in breaking down the Tatar resistance was played by a battery-tower (3). It was built by Ivan Vyrodkov, about

12m high, and contained ten heavy, large-calibre cannon and 50 lighter cannon of smaller calibre. By 1 October, mines had made a considerable breach in the wall of the fortress and on the following day a general assault was undertaken. After a violent battle Kazan was captured. In this plate we can see part of the line of circumvallation, a breach-battery and siege mine. The entire fortress of Kazan was surrounded by siege lines consisting of earth fortifications, a palisade and wicker baskets filled with earth. The besieged are digging a sap under the cover of cannon fire. On the right we can see the entrance to the mine gallery. It was the first recorded instance of a mine gallery being used by Russian troops and the work was carried out under the supervision of the foreign engineer Nemchin Rozmysl (4).

none of them was successful. Not only did the besieged put up a stubborn defence, but they also made three or four sorties every day. At length, the attackers decided to flood the town, which was situated on the bank of a river. A dam about half a kilometre long was built in and the rising water flooded not only the town fortifications but also the kremlin itself. The population sought refuge on the roofs and before long, famine compelled the defenders to surrender.

When they laid a siege the Russians brought massive artillery fire to bear upon enemy fortifications, undertook numerous assaults and even resorted to such methods as the diversion of a river. The method of gradual attack combined with mining was not often employed during the 16th and 17th centuries, though it was used at the sieges of Derpt (1558), Revel (1570) and Riga (1656) and applied to near perfection at the siege of Smolensk in 1632, although Polish reinforcements forced the withdrawal of the Russian Army and the lifting of the siege.

A merlon with a loophole from the Kazan Kremlin. Loopholes in the centre of merlons added to the potential firepower of the defences of the wall.

Aftermath

In 1682 Peter I, widely known as Peter the Great, assumed the throne together with his brother Ivan V. He was then only ten years old and it was the Tsarevna Sofia who really ruled the country. After the death of Ivan V, Peter assumed sole control and his rule (1682–1725) was marked by dramatic changes throughout the country. Amongst the many other reforms, the army was reorganized on a European pattern. The country's fortifications were also updated in a European style and from this date onwards only traced and polygonal fortresses were built.

The role of the kremlin as a town's main defensive citadel had already declined by the beginning of the 17th century. Throughout the course of the century kremlins became symbols of the wealth and rank of towns and they became richly decorated, eventually becoming the seats of governmental offices, cathedrals, state museums and memorials.

The Moscow Kremlin serves as a good example of the fate that befell kremlins in the 17th–20th centuries. In the 17th century almost all the towers of the Kremlin were given pitched roofs, some of them were provided with big clocks, drawbridges were replaced with stationary stone bridges and the purely decorative Tzarskaya Tower was erected on the east side. In 1707–08 in the face of a Swedish threat the Kremlin and adjoining Kitai-Gorod were fortified with earthworks – bastions joined by curtains were put in front of each tower and 1,145 cannon were set up. However, this system of fortifications was never tested in battle, and in 1819–23 it was razed to the ground. The remains of the bastions have only been preserved in the Alexandrovski Garden by the northern wall of the Kremlin.

In 1737 the wooden roof that protected the wall-walk burned down and it was never restored. At the turn of the 19th century all the outer walls of the Kremlin were dismantled and the moats filled up. In 1812 the retreating French Army blew up some of the walls and towers and these were restored in 1816–19. During the Soviet period systematic repair and renovation works were carried on and in 1925 the area along the wall of the Kremlin where it faces Red Square was turned into a burial ground for the most prominent figures of the Communist movement. In 1929 a mausoleum was erected here, in which the body of V. I. Lenin was laid. In 1935–37 the spires of five of the towers were crowned with five-pointed stars.

The Great Kremlin Palace was built inside the Kremlin in 1839–49, the Armoury Chamber was constructed in 1844–51, and in 1959–61 the Kremlin Palace of Congresses was constructed. In 1967 the tomb of the Unknown Soldier with the Eternal Fire and the Guard of Honour in honour of the warriors killed in World War II was placed outside the northern wall.

Other Russian kremlins shared a similar fate – military fortresses were never restored or rebuilt unless they were of great strategic importance. Wooden fortifications have either rotted – if they were out of use – or been replaced by masonry ones, so most of the wooden forts of Siberia (ostrogs) have not survived. A few of the fairly well-preserved towers of those ostrogs have been brought to Moscow and are now exhibited in the Kolomenskoye park. Some masonry fortresses were dismantled once they lost their strategic importance and used as building material by the local population. Even more tragic is the fate of the fortress of Yam-Gorod. This veteran fortress had withstood a number of sieges by Swedish and German armies and was finally dismantled by the order of Catherine II, who, passing by it in 1781, found it too tumbledown and not beautiful enough.

Town defensive walls have also mostly not survived. They lost their defensive role in the 18th century and were often dismantled, ramparts levelled to the ground and moats filled up. Of the Moscow fortifications the outer ring, the Zemlyanoi-Gorod, was the first to disappear. In 1738 the decrepit wooden walls were taken to pieces and in 1816–30 the rampart was razed to the ground and gardens were planted which gave rise to the area's current name Sadovoye Kol'tso (garden ring). Where the gate-towers of Zemlyanoi-Gorod used to stand, squares are now found. The Bely-Gorod was dismantled in the second half of the 18th century and is now the boulevard ring of Moscow. The walls of Kitai-Gorod survived the longest and, although they were built over in the 18th and 19th centuries, they were not demolished until 1934 when the city centre was redeveloped. Some sections of the wall were left as historical monuments and they can be seen today.

Monastery walls were generally constantly renovated and restored. So although they lost their military significance as far back as the 17th century they have served as a public demonstration of the wealth and vitality of the foundation ever since.

The Alexeevskaya Tower of Novgorod the Great. This is the only surviving tower of the *okol'ny gorod*, built in 1582–84.

The sites today

The best time for visiting Russian fortresses is May, June and July. These are the months when the sun shines most frequently. In autumn, early spring and sometimes in August the sky is usually cloudy and it often rains. In winter the fortresses are covered with snow and although they look beautiful, the deep snow and icy slopes may make sightseeing both difficult and dangerous.

All kremlins, fortresses and monasteries are open to visitors. However, in most kremlins and monasteries one can only have a walk along sections of the walls assigned for the purpose. The Moscow Kremlin is the seat of the Russian government and most of the area is closed to visitors. Functioning monasteries and some of the kremlins are only open to visitors at set times, usually in the morning. Urban fortifications and the ruins of some military fortresses standing by themselves can be seen at any time. There is an entrance fee at most kremlins, monasteries and fortresses, which is usually low for Russian citizens but two or three times higher for foreigners.

The better-preserved and most famous kremlins, military fortresses, monasteries and urban defences are listed below.

Kremlins

Kazan

After the Russian armies seized Kazan in 1552, the Tatars' fortifications were replaced by a kremlin. Its fortifications were mostly built around 1555; however, in the 17th and 18th centuries the kremlin was completely reconstructed and the masonry and brick walls were painted white. The walls have now been fully restored. A distinctive feature of the Kazan Kremlin is the mosque – it is the only kremlin to have one – though this mosque was only built in the 20th century.

General view of Ivangorod Fortress. In the centre of the picture one can see the fortifications of Peredni-Gorod (front town), built in 1610. In front of them there is a low embankment faced with masonry, and behind there are the tower and walls of a citadel built in 1507, which was called the Zamok (castle).

Moscow

The fortifications of the Moscow Kremlin have been described in detail above. They were mainly erected in 1485–95 but later redevelopment considerably altered some of the elements. As a symbol not only of Moscow but of the whole of Russia, the Kremlin has been repeatedly renovated, hence its excellent condition today.

Nizhni Novgorod

The kremlin of Nizhni Novgorod has been restored and is in excellent condition.

Novgorod the Great

The fortifications of the kremlin have now been restored and their size is impressive indeed. The Novgorod Kremlin was never besieged during its centuries-old history and its formidable fortifications remain untested.

Tula

The Tula Kremlin is a perfect example of a 'regular' fortification – its straight walls and projecting towers allowed effective flanking fire to be brought to bear on a potential enemy. The stone and brick walls of the kremlin are well preserved.

Military fortresses

Ivangorod

This fortress is situated in the town of Ivangorod, south-west of St Petersburg on the Estonian border. Those planning on visiting Ivangorod should bear in mind that it is now in a frontier zone so special permission from the commandant's office in the town of Kingisepp is needed for those intending to visit.

View through a loophole in the Shirokaya (broad) Tower of Ivangorod. Note how well the entire space at the foot of the wall can be covered by fire.

The parapet of the wall of Ivangorod, shown with the author for scale.

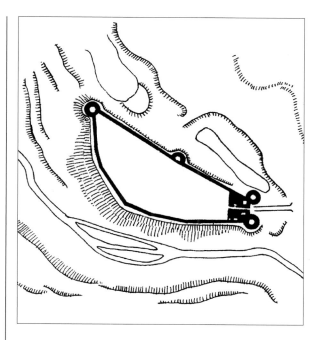

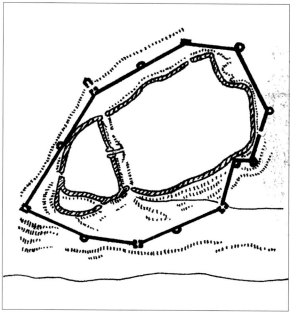

ABOVE LEFT Plan of Kopor'e, 13th–16th centuries. The fortress only has four towers, two of which protect the gates. It stands on a hill and the builders had to conform to the topography, which is why the wall facing the river is curved. Although this meant that flanking fire could not be conducted from this wall, the steep nature of the relief made this a difficult avenue of attack.

ABOVE RIGHT Plan of the kremlin of Nizhni Novgorod. The fortifications one can see here today date back to the early 16th century. The plan shows that the curtains are straight and this enabled the defenders to conduct effective flanking fire.

Kopor'e
The fortress is situated to the west of St Petersburg, 12km from the Gulf of Finland.

Ladoga
The fortress is now to be found in the village of Staraya (Old) Ladoga, 125km to the east of St Petersburg.

Oreshek
The fortress is situated on Orehovy Island, Lake Ladoga, at the source of the Neva River. Only six towers out of ten have been preserved and a few sections of the fortress have been restored.

Monasteries
Pskovo-Pechorski Nunnery
The nunnery is situated in the town of Pechory, 52km west of Pskov. It's a functioning nunnery readily visited by tourists. The fortifications are kept in excellent condition and there is a pleasant park in the area.

Troitse-Sergiev Monastery
Situated to the north-east of Moscow in the town of Sergiev-Possad. In 1744 Empress Elizabeth granted the monastery the dignity of Lavra – the highest rank of monastery. UNESCO has included the Troitse-Sergiev Monastery (Lavra) in the list of World Heritage sites.

Urban fortifications
Moscow
The Moscow Kremlin is certainly the major sight in Moscow but the other urban fortifications are worth seeing, too. Unfortunately, out of the town defensive walls (Kitai-Gorod, Bely-Gorod and Zemlyanoi-Gorod) only a rather small part of the Kitai-Gorod has been preserved. Some sections of the wall with towers can be seen in Revolution Square, behind the Metropol' Hotel and along Kitaigorodski Passage. Some sections of it have swallow's-tail merlons; however, these are not original and were probably added in the 19th century.

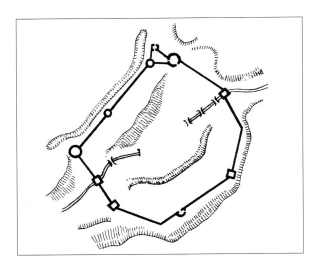

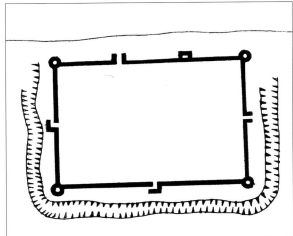

Novgorod the Great
The only elements of the urban defences that survive are the ramparts, moats and the Alekseevskaya Tower, built in 1582–84.

Pskov
Considerable parts of the town fortifications survive, as well as several towers. Among them are the multi-storeyed Gremyach'ya Tower, the low but solid Pokrovskaya Tower, and the ruins of the Varlaamskaya Tower, which are particularly worth seeing. The latter two towers have played an active part in the defence of Pskov and were the target of a great number of enemy assaults. All in all Pskov has withstood 26 sieges during its history.

Smolensk
The lengthy fortifications seen today date from 1595–1602, with only minor alterations from the second half of the 17th century.

ABOVE LEFT Plan of the Pskovo-Pechorski Nunnery, 1553–65. The nunnery stands on the bank of a small river running along a hollow between two hills. As a result, its walls have a unique stepped structure.

ABOVE RIGHT Plan of the Tula Kremlin, 1507–20. As can be seen from the plan, the Tula Kremlin looks like a 'regular' fortress.

BELOW A tower of Kitai-Gorod. This is one of the few surviving towers of the urban fortifications of Moscow.

Bibliography

No comprehensive works on Russian fortresses have so far been published in English. In the books cited below the reader will find short references to some Russian fortresses, fragmentary pieces of information about their construction or just a few photographs:

Duffy, C., *Siege Warfare, The Fortress in the Early Modern World 1494–1660* (London, 1997)

Gravett, C., *The History of Castles, Fortifications around the World* (Guildford, 2001)

Kaufmann, J. E., and Kaufmann, H. W., *The Medieval Fortress* (London, 2001)

Nicolle, D., *Medieval Warfare. Source Book. Christian Europe and its Neighbours* (London, 1998)

Nicolle, D., Shpakovsky V., *Medieval Russian Armies, 1250–1500* (Oxford, 2002)

Oggins, R. S., *Castles and Fortresses* (New York, 1998)

These Russian-language books contain a great deal more detailed information about the fortresses of this period, but are almost impossible to find in the West:

Gulyanitskii, N. F. (ed.) *Drevnerusskoye gradostroitel'stvo X–XV veka* (*Ancient Russian Town-Planning, 10th–15th Centuries*), (Moscow, 1993)

Ivanov, Yu. G., *Velikiye kreposti Rossii* (*The Great Fortresses of Russia*) (Smolensk, 2004)

Ivanova, O. Yu., *Monastyri Rossii* (*Monasteries of Russia*) (Smolensk, 2004)

Kirpichnikov, A. N., *Kamennyye kreposti Novgorodskoy zemli* (*The Stone Fortresses of the Novgorod District*) (Leningrad, 1984)

Kirpichnikov, A. N., 'Kreposti bastionnogo tipa v srednevekovoy Rossii (Bastioned Trace Fortresses in Medieval Russia)', *Pamyatniki kul'tury. Novyye otkrytiya. Pis'mennost'. Iskusstvo. Arkheologiya. Ezhegodnik – 1978* (*Culture Memorials. New Developments. Literary Texts. Art. Archeology. The Yearbook – 1978*) (Leningrad, 1979)

Kostochkin, V. V., *Drevnerusskiye goroda. Pamyatniki zodchestva XI–XVII vekov* (*Ancient Russian Towns. The Monuments of Architecture, 11th–17th Centuries*) (Moscow, 1972)

Kostochkin, V. V., *Drevniye russkiye kreposti* (*Ancient Russian Fortresses*) (Moscow, 1964)

Kostochkin, V. V., *Krepostnoye zodchestvo drevney Rusi* (*The Military Architecture of Ancient Rus*) (Moscow, 1969)

Kostochkin, V. V., *Russkoye oboronnoye zodchestvo kontsa XIII–nachala XVI vekov* (*Russian Defence Architecture, end of the 13th–beginning of the 16th Centuries*) (Moscow, 1962)

Kradin, N. P., *Russkoye derevyannoye oboronnoye zodchestvo* (*Russian Wooden Defence Architecture*) (Moscow, 1988)

Kyui, Ts., *Kratki istoricheski ocherk dolgovremennoi fortifikatsii v Rossii* (*A Short Historical Essay on Long-Term Fortifications in Russia*) (St Petersburg, 1897)

Laskovskii, F., *Materialy dlya Istorii Ingenernogo Iskusstva v Rossii* (*Materials for the History of the Engineering Art in Russia*), 3 vols (St Petersburg, 1858–65)

Nikitin, A. V., 'Oboronitel'nyye sooruzheniya zasechnoy cherty 16-17 vekov (Defensive Works of the Zasechnaya Cherta in the 16th–17th Centuries)', *Materialy i issledovaniya po arkheologii SSSR* (*Materials and Investigations on Archaeology in the USSR*), No. 44, p.116–213 (Moscow, 1955)

Nossov, K. S., *Russkiye kreposti i osadnaya tehnika VIII–XVII vekov* (*Russian Fortresses and Siege Warfare, 8th–17th Centuries*) (St Petersburg and Moscow, 2003)

Rappoport, P. A., *Drevniye russkiye kreposti* (*Ancient Russian Fortresses*) (Moscow, 1965)

Rappoport, P. A., 'Ocherki po istorii voyennogo zodchestva Severo-Vostochnoy i Severo-Zapadnoy Rusi X–XV vekov (Essays on the History of Military Architecture of North-East and North-West Rus', 10th–15th Centuries)', *Materialy i issledovaniya po arkheologii SSSR* (*Materials and Investigations on Archaeology in the USSR*), No. 105, p.1–244 (Moscow and Leningrad, 1961)

Yakovlev, A. I., *Zasechnaya cherta Moskovskogo gosudarstva v XVII veke* (*Zasechnaya Cherta of Moscow State in the 17th Century*) (Moscow, 1916)

Glossary

bashnya Tower. The term appeared in the 16th century and replaced the terms *kostyor* and *strel'nitsa*.

boevoy hod An open or closed gallery stretching out along the top of the wall by the parapet (wall-walk).

chastokol A wall of wooden stakes arranged, vertically or obliquely, in a row (palisade).

detinets Citadel. The term was widely used up to the 14th century; later it was used in the Novgorod the Great region and was replaced by the term kremlin in the Moscow and Tver principalities and by the term *krom* in the Pskov principality.

gorod Defensive walls, a fortress.

gorodni Cells (log framework) of a wooden wall in ancient Russian fortifications put edge to edge but not joined to each other.

gorodnik A military engineer in charge of the building of fortifications.

kosoi ostrog A palisade that had a slope in the direction of the enclosed space.

kostyor The name for a tower, common in the Pskov and Novgorod the Great regions until the 16th century.

kremlin Fortress in a city (citadel). The term appeared in the 14th century and replaced the earlier term *detinets* in the Moscow and Tver principalities.

krepost' Fortress. The term appeared in the 17th century in place of the earlier term *gorod*.

krom Citadel. The term appeared in the 14th century and was used in the Pskov principality instead of the earlier term *detinets*.

krovat' A wooden planking (wall-walk) by a palisade wall.

nadolby A barrier made of logs dug into the ground with a slope in the direction of the enemy.

nadvratnaya bashnya Gate-tower.

oblam (oblom) An overhanging projection in the upper part of a wooden wall or a tower, a kind of a machicolation. Sometimes used as a synonym of *zaborola*.

okol'ny gorod The external line of the town walls.

osadnaya klet' A very small room in a kremlin to live in or keep valuables during a siege (common people).

osadny dvor A small room in a kremlin to live in or keep valuables during a siege (nobility and clergy).

ostrog A small fortified settlement surrounded by wooden walls; also an external line of town fortifications; it was also used in the sense of *tyn* (palisade).

osyp' Earthen rampart.

otvodnaya strel'nitsa A bridgehead fortress tower that served to fortify the defence of the *nadvratnaya bashnya*.

pechura A box-room with an embrasure, for placing a cannon in a tower or a wall.

podoshvenny boy The lower tier of loopholes and embrasures at the foot of a wall.

polati Wall-walk of a palisade wall, the same as *krovat'*.

possad A settlement populated by craftsmen and traders outside the walls of the kremlin.

prikladka External masonry erected for the purpose of fortifying a wall.

pryaslo The part of a fortress wall between two towers (curtain).

raskat A small site meant for mounting cannon; it is also used in the sense of a bastion.

shlyah A road along which the Tatars made their raids.

sluh An underground passage leading beyond the defensive wall and used for the detection of sapping work by the enemy.

sredni boy The middle tier of loopholes and embrasures in the wall.

storozhy Small fortified observation posts situated on raised ground, commonly seen in the 15th–17th centuries.

stoyachi ostrog A vertical palisade.

strel'nitsa A name of a tower common in the Moscow district until the 16th century.

tainichnaya (also tainitskaya) bashnya A tower where the entrance to a *tainik* was situated.

tainik An arrangement for supplying the fortress with water. It was an underground corridor leading out of the fortress and down the slope of a hill to a level where it was easy to dig a well.

tarassy The structure of log walls with longitudinal logs overlapping each other with the help of single cross-wise walls. Unlike the *gorodni* the *tarassy* structure was a solid wall, not separate cells joined together.

tur Gabion.

tyn See *chastokol*.

tyufyak A small cannon of the howitzer type.

'v kletku' A wooden wall of the *tarassy* structure, the inner space of which is not filled with earth or clay.

'v lapu' The way of joining logs at the corners so that their ends did not stick out beyond the external surface of the wall.

'v oblo' The way of joining logs at the corners so that their ends stuck out beyond the external surface of the wall.

varovy boy Machicolation.

voivode The commander of an army or governor of a province in medieval Russia.

zaborola (zabrala) The projecting upper part of a wall covered with a roof and overhanging the lower part of the wall (like hoarding). The term is sometimes considered as a synonym of *oblam* or even of a wall in general.

zakhab A specific type of barbican.

zaseka Heaps of slashed trees cut in such a way that their tops and branches jut in the direction of the enemy.

zimov'e A small fortress in the early period of the development of Siberia.

Index

Figures in **bold** refer to illustrations